29/06

Architect's Essentials of Presentation Skills

Architect's Essentials of Presentation Skills

David Greusel, AIA

John Wiley & Sons, Inc.

Copyright © 2002 by John Wiley & Sons, Inc., New York.
All rights reserved.

Published simultaneously in Canada.

This publication is designed to provide accurate and authoritative
information in regard to the subject matter covered. It is sold with
the understanding that the publisher is not engaged in rendering
professional services. If professional advice or other expert assistance
is required, the services of a competent professional person should be
sought.

Wiley also publishes its books in a variety of electronic formats. Some
content that appears in print may not be available in electronic books.
For more information about Wiley products, visit our web site at
www.wiley.com.

AIA, The American Institute of Architects, and the AIA logo are
registered trademarks and service marks of The American Institute
of Architects.

Library of Congress Cataloging-in-Publication Data:

Greusel, David.
 Architect's essentials of presentation skills / David Greusel.
   p.   cm.
 ISBN 0-471-17675-3 (alk. paper)
 1. Public speaking. 2. Architects. I. Title.
 PN4192.A72 G74 2002
 808.5′1—dc21

                                                    2002003826

PRINTED IN THE UNITED STATES OF AMERICA.
10 9 8 7 6 5 4 3 2 1

*This book is dedicated
to my beloved bride,
Theresa,
without whose love and support
the author would be both
a worse presenter and a worse person.*

Contents

2
What's My Motivation?

3
Know Your Lines

4
Find Your Light

PART II
DELIVERING YOUR PRESENTATION

Foreword

As recently as May 2002, surveys by The American Institute of Architects reinforce a disturbing fact of modern practice: Our clients and the broader public whom we serve do not understand *what* we do as architects nor *how* we do it. Responses from a wide spectrum of clients suggest that they define design as a *noun*; to them, design is valued as a product or object. By contrast, architects define design as a *verb*; a creative, right-brain process that is nonlinear, interactive, interdisciplinary, integrated yet responsive to a client and community.

Should we worry about this disconnect? Should we care that the expectations of the client and the architect are not aligned? The answer is a resounding *Yes!* Without clarity of expectation and alignment of understanding, it is difficult to establish value, difficult to create meaningful projects, and difficult to arrive at a shared perspective of what is appropriate compensation.

Little wonder that given the lack of understanding of *what* we do, *how* we do it, *what* to expect, and *how* to define value, trust has emerged as a decisive factor in how clients select their architect. Therefore, one could make the case that part of the core curriculum of an architect's schooling should be how to design, develop, and communicate trust, through both the design and the communication processes. Instead, we are taught to base our credibility and worth on our mastery of technical skills, skills that are imperfectly understood by our clients.

As an architect, I am disturbed by what these surveys are telling us. But, then, why should I be? After all, I have no idea how to identify a first-rate cardiac surgeon other than by sensing—from my communication with the surgeon—whether he or she inspires a high level of confidence and trust. Building trust occurs daily, every hour, and with everyone with whom we interact. Whether or not we are aware of it, all of us are in fact marketing and presenting ourselves every minute of the day in a variety of engagements. For an architect, no professional engagement is more important than the formal presentations needed to acquire a commission. These presentations are not only key to distinguishing one firm from another, they also lay the groundwork for the ongoing relationship with the client and the ultimate success of the project.

All of this is to say that David Greusel's book, *Architect's Essentials of Presentation Skills*, focuses on one of the most important issues facing modern architecture practice. Anyone who has sat in on the selection side of a presentation will recall how easily things can go terribly wrong: Boredom begins to set in; from boredom comes impatience; from impatience comes antagonism; from antagonism comes negativity, and finally rejection.

As Greusel notes: "Architects...mistakenly assume that their work will speak for itself." Unfortunately for the architect, as Greusel goes on to note, the individuals to whom we are making the presentation (clients) are typically left-brain (verbal and analytical) thinkers while architects are primarily gifted with right-brain (visual and graphic) abilities. Thus, how naive of us to think that our work will speak for itself. To back up his point, Greusel offers a "message erosion" diagram that identifies the misalignment among (1) what we meant to say, (2) what we actually said, (3) what the listener heard, and (4) what the listener understood. We may think we are speaking with the tongues of angels, but Greusel cites experts who estimate that as much as 80 percent of spoken messages are lost en route from speaker to listener.

The issue is enormous in its implications, and a book that tackles the entire spectrum of communication and relationship building remains to be written. Greusel has taken a giant first step, and I applaud his ability to remain focused on the need to cover comprehensively the issues related to getting the job. His Ten Commandments of effective presentations are obviously based on firsthand experience. I most appreciate his willingness to identify the problem without dictating a single right answer; leaving the search for a right answer to the individual reader to determine. Clearly a book of best practice!

Gordon H. Chong, FAIA
President
The American Institute of Architects

Partner
Gordon H. Chong & Partners
San Francisco

Acknowledgments

Most of the ideas found in this book originated from my experiences of some 28 years in the performing arts. As such, I am indebted to many of the directors with whom I have had the privilege of working, including Peter Mann Smith, Lew Shelton, Lynn Barbara Mahler, Carl Hinrichs, Mary Jane Teall, Knox Nimock, and Darrell Brogdon, among others, for helping me learn the rules of the stage. I am also grateful to The American Institute of Architects for providing the forum in which my theories about "architecture as performance art" have been refined, and to HOK Sport + Venue + Event for providing me the latitude to pursue this area of professional interest. Thanks are due to Margaret Cummins of John Wiley & Sons for encouraging me to undertake this project. And, ultimately, I acknowledge with profound gratitude the Audience of One before whom we all perform.

Architect's Essentials of Presentation Skills

Introduction: Design Professionals and Presentations

Reality Check

Other than oral surgery, there are few things people dread more than having to make oral presentations. There is ample evidence to suggest that many people fear death less than they do public speaking. Yet making oral presentations is a major part of almost every design professional's life. Curiously, learning how to make effective presentations is seldom a part of any design professional's training, either in school or after. This paradox has led to the creation of this book, which is intended to give you some practical tools and advice for making the best presentations possible.

Most professionals have been subjected to awful presentations at some point in their careers, and design professionals are no exception. There are several reasons for this fact:

> ➤ As with any activity, we tend not to do well what we've not been trained to do at all.

> ➤ Architects and designers tend to be right-brained (visual and graphic) rather than left-

brained (verbal and analytical) thinkers. This leads, quite naturally, to graphic excellence and verbal and analytical mediocrity.

► Perhaps because of the latter, speech, theater, debate, and drama are subjects that designers avoid studying and participating in throughout their secondary and college educations.

► Most designers work right up to the last minute on the graphic part of an assignment (this is as true out of school as it is in college), and leave themselves little or no time to plan the oral presentation of their work.

► Architects, like many people, mistakenly assume that their work will speak for itself.

► Like many people, design professionals can underestimate the emotional factors that influence presentations until they are giving the presentations, at which point it's too late to do anything about them.

► Having lived with a project or proposal for days or weeks, designers mistakenly assume that they will be able to converse about it knowledgeably and intelligently with little preparation.

► Ironically, despite their spatial reasoning ability, which is obviously above the norm, architects have little sense of the space their own bodies occupy, and how to work within it.

Regardless of the reasons, the unpleasant reality of sitting through a stiff, boring, incoherent presentation by oneself or others should be enough to drive massive sales of this book in the design professions, if it provides anything of value in the prevention of such experiences. This volume is intended to cover

Introduction: Design Professionals and Presentations

the basic essentials of presenting from the point of view of practicing architects and design professionals in real-life situations. As such, it should be useful to anyone in the design professions for whom presenting is a part of the job description—which is to say, nearly everyone. The lessons contained here have been gleaned from more than 25 years' experience in both architecture and the performing arts, and from several years of having presented a seminar on this topic to the national convention of The American Institute of Architects (AIA). They have also been proven (or shown to be necessary by their omission) in hundreds of marketing and design presentations given or observed by the author.

Speaking of marketing, a disclaimer of purpose is important here: As stated above, the intention of this book is to help you make the most effective presentations possible. That is related to, but not exactly the same as, winning a marketing effort. Although presenting is a crucial element of marketing, any good marketer will confirm that it is not the only element—and in many cases, not even the most important element. Improving your presentation skills will help you get work, but it will not by itself get you work. It is entirely possible (and we have all seen it happen) to win the presentation and lose the job for entirely different reasons. So you should consider effective presentation skills an important weapon in your marketing arsenal, but not the solution to all your marketing problems.

REMINDER

A winning presentation is not the same as a winning marketing effort: Success is getting your message across whether you get the job or not.

Defining Success

It might be useful, in light of the preceding, to define what success means in the context of this book. Since winning projects and clients often depends on many other factors besides giving the best presentation, how can we define a successful presentation? One view is that a successful presentation is one in which the core message is effectively communicated to the intended audience.

This is not as simple as it sounds. There are many roadblocks that inhibit the successful receipt of a message communicated orally (see Figure I.1). Among these are the speaker's inability to say what he or she is thinking, environmental factors (ambient noise or other distractions), and the listener's inability to effectively process both the language and the contextual cues that are part of the total communication. Taken together, some experts estimate that as much of 80 percent of spoken messages are lost en route from speaker to listener. If you think back to the last time you heard someone give a talk and estimate how much of that talk you actually remember, it becomes clear that 80 percent may be an optimistic figure.

In light of the fact that marketing success cannot be guaranteed by even the best presentation, it seems reasonable, then, to define success in other terms. The terms suggested here are that if you have effectively communicated what you want your listeners

RULE OF THUMB

Eighty percent of oral communication is lost to the audience or listener within hours of a presentation.

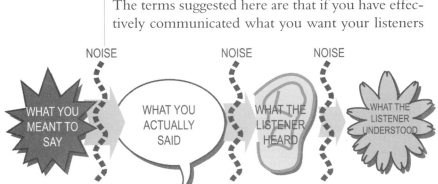

Figure I.1 The communication process—message erosion.

Introduction: Design Professionals and Presentations

Your Worst Nightmares

In the process of teaching a seminar on presentation skills to groups of architects and others over the past several years, the audience has been polled on the greatest presentation fears that people have. The list has remained remarkably consistent from group to group and from year to year. What people fear most in making oral presentations is

- ▶ *Not knowing what to say.* That sense, usually born of a lack of preparation, that while the work may be worth presenting, when the moment of truth arrives, the words to describe it won't be there.

- ▶ *Being boring.* The fear that while you know your stuff, it may not be interesting enough to keep your audience fully engaged for the duration of your talk.

- ▶ *Forgetting what you had planned to say.* The slightly panicky feeling of being onstage and not remembering your lines.

- ▶ *Facing a hostile audience.* Often the case in zoning and other public hearings, the fear that either the governing body or the audience will be openly hostile to the cause you are advocating. Accompanying this fear is not just the fear of failing to accomplish the mission, but also the fear of how you are going to deal with hostile questions (and questioners).

- ▶ *Experiencing technical difficulties.* The pervasive fear that some piece of critical technology (in earlier times, the slide projector) will fail at a critical moment.

- ▶ *Being in an unsuitable environment.* The concern that a presentation will occur in a space that is too large, too small, or (often the case) too bright for the activity you have planned.

- ▶ *Experiencing stage fright.* That all-encompassing nervous tension that creates galloping hearts, shortness of breath, jittery knees, flip-flopping stomachs, and uncontrolled sweating when you stand up to present.

- ▶ *Fielding hard questions.* Related to "not knowing what to say," this fear anticipates the part of a presentation that is out of your control: the question-and-answer session, and the difficulty of predicting what questions will be asked. This makes it hard to have coherent answers ready.

- ▶ *Failing to control or manage co-presenters.* Many presenters fear their colleagues most of all, thinking, "I know I can do what's needed, but Mr. Colleague never rehearses; he just gets up there and does his thing. How can I manage to keep him from going overtime or off the subject?"

While this list is hardly exhaustive, it covers the primary fears of architects and designers in making presentations. And, as you review the list, you can see that most of those fears are well founded, given the lack of training and experience most of us have in this area. Moreover, given the competitive climate in which we operate, hostile or nonresponsive audiences are often a very real possibility as well. Dealing with each of these fears in a positive way is one of the fundamental purposes of this book. As you move through the following chapters, you will learn clear, positive steps you can take to overcome each of these problems. Don't worry about finding the magic bullet that solves them all with a single stroke—as any architect knows, different problems require unique solutions—otherwise, design professionals wouldn't have much to do!

to know, think, or believe about you, your firm, or your work, you have made a successful presentation. There are many presentations where the marketing objective may be unattainable, but the communication objective is always obtainable—if you have prepared yourself with the essential skills of a presenter.

Basic Training

As stated above, the purpose of this book is to give you the essential skills and tools you need to make effective presentations about yourself, your firm, or your work in a variety of public and nonpublic settings. In this book, you will learn:

- ▶ The essentials of planning and delivering a presentation
- ▶ Keys to making the most of the time you have available
- ▶ Obvious (and not-so-obvious) mistakes architects frequently make in presentations
- ▶ Ways to engage and entertain your audience
- ▶ Techniques to counteract boredom
- ▶ How to overcome problems when giving a presentation
- ▶ How to maintain your focus
- ▶ What "stage presence" is and how to use it
- ▶ How to overcome tension and stage fright
- ▶ How to manage presentations with multiple presenters
- ▶ How to choose the best visual aids for your presentation
- ▶ How to leave your audience wanting more

While it sounds like a tall order, these attitudes and skills are not difficult to master. But they do require advance preparation. The fact that you are thinking enough about sharpening your presentation skills to have started this book is a sign that better presentations are in your future.

This book is loosely structured around some basic rules of show business (after all, what is a presentation if not a microcosm of show business?) gleaned from over 25 years' experience in the performing arts. These rules are not codified anywhere—it is doubtful that they even exist on a Web site somewhere—but are the result of learning from a lot of different directors and stage managers in a lot of different venues. So without further ado, here are…

The Ten Commandments of Presenting

It may very well be that there are eleven, or fifteen, or five commandments of presenting that would capture the ideas contained in this book just as well, but ten commandments is a well-established paradigm in western culture, and the structure has worked well in the past. A few chapters are tacked on at the end of this book to deal with issues that are larger than the presentation itself, but for the most part, each commandment will be dealt with as a separate chapter. Also, each commandment deals with one (or more) of the worst presentation fears outlined previously, although you will not find a one-to-one correspondence between the fear and the commandment. Of course, the term "commandment" here is used with a certain glibness, as there are neither moral nor ethical issues involved. We are not dealing here with questions of ultimate good and evil, just with the difference between bad and good presentations.

The Ten Commandments of Presenting are listed below, with a brief description of each. Although each commandment is itself a show-business axiom, the discussion of it in the context of this book is more about architectural presentation than about show business. Examples used, however, will be divided between illustrations from performing arts and professional practice.

TEN COMMANDMENTS OF PRESENTING

1. **Show Up.** An investigation of the physical quality of presentations, use of the body, stage presence, and a discussion of appropriate movement.

2. **What's My Motivation?** Understanding the goal of your presentation and how to use that goal to motivate every statement, visual image, and action request in your presentation.

3. **Know Your Lines.** A discussion of the importance of preparation in delivering successful and compelling presentations, and, especially, on the distinction between preparing and rehearsing. Here you will discover the two keys to winning presentations: mastery of the topic, and the paradox of practicing.

4. **Find Your Light.** Looking at the physical environment in which a presentation is to occur, preparing the space, and preparing yourself to be seen and heard in it.

5. **Face Out.** A discussion of five aspects of presenting that keep audiences involved: energy, empathy, engagement, enthusiasm, and entertainment.

6. **Keep Going.** Dealing with obstacles and breakdowns in a presentation, especially when your options are limited.
7. **Project.** How to make yourself heard in different presentation venues.
8. **Be in the Moment.** A discussion of focus and concentration and the importance of maintaining intensity at the time of your presentation.
9. **Remember Your Props.** Consideration of various types of visual aids used by architects, and their pluses and minuses.
10. **Know When to Get Off.** How pace and timing affect the delivery of a presentation, as well as a discussion of stage management techniques and managing multiple presenters.

These commandments have been proven over and over, not only in the performing arts, but in the arena of professional presentations, and they work. They have also been overlooked and forgotten on numerous occasions, and on each such occasion, their absence has been noteworthy. They constitute the best available guidelines not for life (as with the original Ten Commandments), but for making effective presentations. Ignore them at your peril.

Planning and Preparation

Part I

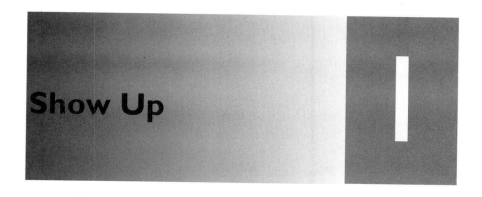

Show Up

"*Eighty percent of success is just showing up.*"
— WOODY ALLEN

Obviously, no professional worthy of the title would fail to show up for a presentation, barring a personal emergency or natural disaster, right? So what could possibly be the relevance of a commandment to show up? This first, and most crucial, commandment originates with a theatrical director who instructed his actors on the first day of rehearsals that failure to show up, or even tardiness, would result in immediate dismissal from the production. You can imagine the galvanizing effect this edict had on the cast. Were any of the actors ever late for rehearsal or absent altogether? Not one. Yet, amazingly, some architects and designers so overschedule their work life that making it to a presentation on time is not a given, more of a hopeful desire. So even though it should go without saying, the first part of showing up is showing up, on time and prepared to present.

The notion of being prepared has several aspects, which will be explored in some depth. But of primary importance is physical and mental preparation, which has to do with getting your body and your mind in the right attitude to present. This is not a trivial issue, as anyone who has watched design professionals present can attest.

Physical Preparation

One realization that comes late to many presenters, if it comes at all, is the inescapable fact that presenting is first and foremost a physical activity. Many professionals are under the mistaken impression that oral presentations are just an inefficient way to download intellectual content to a group—an activity that could be accomplished much more effectively with a memorandum, or perhaps a drawing.

They couldn't be more wrong. Oral presentations are first and foremost a performance. Your audience, whether it is a committee, a board, or a group of colleagues, is there to see you perform, preferably on your feet. Their evaluation of your performance has everything to do with the degree to which you are physically present, physically aware, and physically in control.

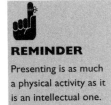

REMINDER

Presenting is as much a physical activity as it is an intellectual one.

Presenting is more like dance than it is like reading a memo aloud. That doesn't mean you need to learn the waltz or the Watusi; it means you need to be prepared to engage the physical nature of the activity. More will be said about this in the section on stage presence in this chapter.

Physical preparation requires that your body be warmed up and loose for a presentation—just as if you were preparing to run a road race, play tennis, or work in your garden. Actors warm up their bodies before each rehearsal and each performance. Most presenters don't get past doing a deep-breathing exercise in their warm-up routine—not a particularly helpful thing in itself, as will be discussed later, but also inadequate to the task.

There are a number of things you can do to physically warm up for a presentation, even if you are wearing a business suit, and even if you are in the company of colleagues among whom you don't wish to be thought insane. Warming up does not require doing jumping jacks or wind sprints, you'll be relieved to hear.

The first thing you need to do to warm up is to take inventory. This means asking yourself these questions: "How am I feeling right now? Am I completely physically relaxed?" If you're honest, the answer is probably no. Next you need to localize the area(s) of tension in your body. Is it your stomach? Your back? Your neck? Upper arms? Wherever you feel tense, you need to isolate that area to relax it. The most effective way to deal with tension (without doing jumping jacks) is through isometrics. Isometric exercise simply pits one muscle group against another in a static tug of war that doesn't require any actual movement. If it sounds a little improbable, picture an arm-wrestling contest in a bar. If the two contestants are evenly matched (isometric), there will be amazingly little movement even though both contestants are straining with all their might.

Isometrics are also called tension-relaxation exercises, not because they relax tension (which they do), but because they cycle from tension to relaxation and back again several times. If you are sitting down (or not), you can do this exercise right now, without anyone being able to observe it (unless you tend to

RULE OF THUMB

Part of physical preparation is being aware of your own body and how it is feeling at the time of your presentation.

Show Up

get red in the face). Try scrunching up your toes inside your shoe—right now. Hold it for five seconds, then release. Then do it again. That, in essence, is the tension-relaxation exercise. Because it's isometric, it doesn't require any significant movement. Now try it with some other muscle groups. Try isolating your thigh muscles, or your lower back, or your shoulders. Some muscle groups are hard to find (calves, for example)—not anatomically, obviously, but isometrically. But with a small amount of practice, you can isolate and tense just about any muscle group in your body.

The advantage of isometric tension-relaxation exercise, besides the previously mentioned fact that it doesn't require you to jump around, is that it allows you to work with the tension you naturally have prior to a presentation and overcome it. This is much more effective than wishing it away ("I wish I were more relaxed right now") or denying it exists. And if you start with the areas where you feel the most tension, you'll do yourself the most good just prior to beginning your presentation.

Does isometric exercise get rid of tension entirely? No. But it will help you to manage the tension that presenters naturally feel before going on, and it will help you be aware of your body and its signals to you as you begin your presentation.

So what about deep breathing—the prescription most often given for prepresentation tension (also known as stage fright)? Does it do any good? Deep breathing is better than doing nothing, but not much. For one thing, nervous people breathing deeply can easily hyperventilate (breathe too much, too fast). This is obviously not helpful. But being aware of your breathing pattern is useful and important, as will be discussed later in Chapter 7, "Project."

WARNING!
Avoid deep breathing as part of your warm-up routine: It can make you lightheaded.

Show Up

Other activities that can be helpful for physically warming you up to present include:

➤ Walk the last few blocks to the presentation site. You'll feel warmer, looser, and more sanguine.

➤ If your presentation site is on the second or third floor, climb the stairs to get there. If it's on the thirtieth floor, forget it.

➤ Pacing before a presentation can actually be a good thing—better than pacing during your talk, at any rate. Anything that gets your blood circulating is helpful.

➤ Of course, you don't want to eat a heavy meal just before you present—who could? Most presenters, in warriorlike fashion, refuse to eat at all before their presentation. But a light snack of easily digestible food (a piece of fruit, for example), can help settle your stomach and ease your mind.

➤ If you are able to manage it, doing some kind of workout the day of your presentation will help a lot.

In summary, remember that a presentation is a dance—and you are the dancer. The audience wants to see how you move—not that you need to be fluid and graceful like Fred Astaire, but just that you are in command of your own physicality. In order to be an effective presenter, you must be physically ready to present.

Mental Preparation

In addition to the physical nature of presenting, showing up requires mental preparation. This involves more than just being comfortable with the content of your talk, which will be covered under Commandment 3, "Know Your Lines." Mental preparation is the psychological equivalent of the physical warm-up described above, and just as important.

Check Your Issues at the Door

Of paramount importance in showing up, mentally, for a presentation is the ability to leave your emotional baggage outside the room where the presentation is to take place. Checking your issues, like checking your coat, is a conscious act, and requires you to surrender a small amount of control. Presenters are human, and as such, are subject to any number of physical, psychological, and emotional issues affecting their performance. Most design professionals have more than one project, or potential project, to think about in any given day, not to mention office issues, family, or personal issues. One of the marks of a true professional is his or her ability to overcome those issues when it is time to take the stage and make a presentation.

TIP

Check your issues at the door. Make a conscious decision not to let things you can't control affect your performance.

Checking your issues at the door is making a conscious decision not to let things you cannot control or change affect your performance as a presenter. It means giving up, at least for an hour or two, even the hope of solving whatever other problems may be weighing on you as you prepare to present. At a practical level, it means not writing notes to yourself or your colleagues during a presentation (about other topics), not daydreaming, not wondering where you'll be having lunch after the meeting, and not checking your e-mail on your wireless telecommunications device. Showing up mentally requires your total intellectual participation in the task at hand, which is making a presentation.

In the movie *For Love of the Game*, the baseball player played by Kevin Costner gives us a graphic picture of how to check your issues at the door. As he prepares to deliver his first pitch, Costner's character says to himself, "Clear the mechanism," at which point all the external facets of the game, the stadium, the spectators, the coaches, even the hitter, become invisible, leaving only the catcher's mitt in his conscious mind. Presenters, like this fictional ballplayer, need to be able to "clear the mechanism" before each presentation, focusing not on a catcher's mitt but on the objective of the presentation, which will be discussed in the next chapter.

Stage Presence

It is often remarked of certain actors that they exhibit a wonderful "stage presence," although the thought is seldom carried further to quantify just what that phrase represents. Stage presence is not the exclusive province of actors. But it is a quality worth cultivating.

So what, really, is stage presence? It is the particular way in which a person (usually an actor, but not necessarily) inhabits the space available to him or her. Stage presence relates to movement, which is discussed below, but it is not just about movement. It is possible to have stage presence without moving at all. What is required is that the person (actor or presenter) can command the space they inhabit.

REMINDER

"Stage presence" is simply taking command of the space you have available to you.

A reasonable question at this point is, "Fine, command the space: just how does one do that?" One way to answer this question is to look at how *not* to command the space. The presenter without stage presence is timid, reluctant, a literal wallflower who keeps to the shadows, hides behind the lectern, and generally wishes not to be seen. At its worst, the presenter lacking stage presence can be seen shrinking into his or her own clothing, as though wishing to disappear altogether.

A confident presenter, on the other hand, stands tall (if standing is appropriate), holds his or her head high, and seems willing to take ownership of the room he or she is presenting in.

A simple exercise can help you discern your own level of stage presence. Consider your present posture—probably seated, in a fairly relaxed position. Now imagine that a string is attached to the top of your head. Now pretend that the string is being pulled tight, vertically, lifting your head to the highest possible position without it detaching from your neck. While it may seem awkward at first, this upright position of the head is critical to achieving stage presence. When the head is held aloft (as if by this imaginary string), the rest of the body will naturally fall into a position of alertness that will communicate confidence to the audience. This is true regardless of whether the speaker is seated or standing.

TIP

Pull yourself up from the top of your head (like a marionette) for good posture.

Actors, it will be noted, don't always carry their heads this way, but they *start* this way, and then allow the string to incline them toward or away from other characters or situations as the script dictates. But for the purpose of presenting, it is sufficient for you to practice the string pulling your head vertically, and noting the effect of this action on the rest of your body.

There are other cues that will help you discern whether you have stage presence. It's important to recognize that stage presence is a skill, not a genetic gift or a talent. Just because talented people seem to have it doesn't mean that stage presence is the exclusive domain of the innately talented.

Show Up

Posture, as noted above, is critical. In addition to the "string-from-the-head" technique, which is fundamental, consider the position of your shoulders. If your shoulders are hunched forward as you talk, you are trying to disappear. If your shoulders are thrown back and your chest is out, you may appear pompous or overbearing. But as you can guess, if you have to err, err on the side of shoulders too far back instead of too far forward. Hips, likewise, communicate confidence, or the lack of it. Generally, your hips should be squared up with your shoulders, not cocked at an extreme angle like a mime resting on an imaginary garden wall. Stand in front of a full-length mirror at some point and just study your physical posture: note the position of your shoulders, hips, feet, and hands.

Hands are a critical component of stage presence, because they tell so much about your state of mind. Nervous hand-wringing should obviously be avoided (yet it's surprising how often it can be observed in presenters). So should adopting what comedian Robin Williams calls the "fig leaf position"—hands joined in front of you where they naturally meet—at your crotch. But you can't just let your arms dangle motionless at your sides, either—that looks passive and frightened. Your hands should be part of your presentation toolkit, not useless appendages that get in the way of delivering intellectual content. One hand in a pocket is acceptable; two hands in two pockets makes you look unconfident—or just silly. Spend a few moments thinking about what a relaxed hand position feels like for you. What does a relaxed hand look like on a tabletop? In a standing position? Pointing to something?

All this discussion of particular physical postures related to stage presence is like getting a golf lesson. As you attempt to internalize all the various messages in this section, you may find yourself getting so wrapped up and knotted that giving a talk—like hitting a golf ball—seems impossible. You can't practice all these ideas at the same time—at least not at first—but they are included here for you to refer to as you build your own confident stage persona for presenting.

Most critical of all, however, is the realization that the persona you are building is not a mannequin. As discussed at the beginning of this chapter, presenting is performing, and your audience is waiting to see how you move. Which brings us to the most important element of showing up.

Appropriate Movement

"Movement never lies."
—MARTHA GRAHAM

Ask yourself this question: When you watch speakers give a live presentation, at meetings, rallies, religious services, seminars, anywhere, do you think that they generally move around too much? For most people, the answer is definitely no. Now ask the same question, but relate it specifically to design professionals and their presentations: Do they move around too much? Again, most would say that design professionals do not. Do they move around too little? Such a conclusion might logically follow. So let's think for a moment about how people move—or don't move—in presentations.

Generally, people move when they get up to speak, when they gesture at an exhibit, and when they are done talking. Other than absolutely necessary movement, most speakers stay rooted to one spot. The obvious exceptions to this are the people who nervously sway back and forth or shift their weight from one foot to the other while they speak. We will consider these habits shortly. But, in general, it's clear that most speakers *don't* move too much when they are speaking. In fact, it could be asserted that they don't move enough.

Again, presenting effectively is a dance. It is not a waltz, or a foxtrot, or a break dance, or a ballet, but it is a dance nevertheless. As was mentioned in the discussion of stage presence, your audience wants to see how you move, how you inhabit the space around you, how you interact with other persons on your team and other persons in the room. This dance, and the awareness of its importance, is the critical ingredient to appropriate movement.

There are several impediments to doing the dance well. One of these is well-intentioned advice, sometimes given by expert presenters or speech coaches, to stand with your feet shoulder-width apart, toes slightly outward. Such a posture suggests steadiness and reliability, but it does not suggest that you are ready to dance. Your initial posture, if you even have an initial posture, should be to have one foot slightly ahead of the other, which creates the opportunity, even the impetus, to move.

Another obstacle, one of the most formidable, is the dreaded lectern. The lectern (or podium) is the chief enemy of good presentations, and should be treated as such. There are times, such as a public hearing before a city commission, where the lectern cannot be avoided for reasons having to do with decorum or tape recording (or both), but in every

WARNING!

The lectern is your enemy and should be avoided whenever possible.

case where it can be avoided, you should stay away from lecterns. The lectern invites you to lecture (note the similarity of the noun and verb), not to relate to your audience. And, of course, it's very difficult to dance for your audience when your hands are locked in an icy death grip on the sides of a lectern.

A related issue is the question of the use of microphones, which are becoming more prevalent at public meetings of all kinds. Either this is because the public is becoming progressively more hard of hearing with each passing year or, more likely, because speakers are becoming increasingly reliant on sound amplification to be heard. Whatever the case (the question of how to be heard will be dealt with specifically in Chapter 7), the microphone is not your enemy unless it is rooted to a lectern, in which case it is an accomplice. A wireless microphone can be your friend, and a handheld mike is not necessarily a bad thing (though you need to hold it properly, which will be discussed in Chapter 7 as well). Just don't let the presence of a microphone inhibit your ability to move.

Presenting in too small a room can also inhibit appropriate movement. Many presentations are scheduled in conference rooms designed for seated discussions, not stand-up presenting. In these kinds of rooms, there is often barely enough room behind the overly comfortable conference chairs to move between the chair and the wall, or even worse, your exhibits on tripods. You will need to work hard in such a room to carve out a small piece of terrain on which to perform your dance.

In such a case, it may be advisable to give the entire presentation sitting down. This can be a good idea for reasons of empathy and engagement, which will be discussed in Chapter 5, "Face Out." The disadvantage to a seated presentation it that it limits you to using only half your body to communicate, a real disadvantage. In a very small conference room, this may be your only choice, but give careful thought to the disadvantages before deciding on a seated presentation.

Getting out from behind a lectern raises another question: what to do with your notes. As will be seen in Chapter 3, "Know Your Lines," the best way to speak is without notes, but this approach requires discipline and practice, and may be impossible in some situations. It is sufficient for this discussion to say that, when you move, your notes should move with you, unless you feel confident that you will refer to them only very seldom. Otherwise, think of a format for notes that allows them to be portable. The time-tested 3-by-5 inch index card is a good medium for notes—loose sheets of 8½-by-11 inch paper are not. Some presenters use a legal pad, which is preferable to easily disorganized loose paper.

So what does appropriate movement really look like? Like dancing without music. It means moving in the rhythm of your content, in and out with the points you're trying to make. You can move in to create intensity and emphasis (or lean in if you're seated). You can move out to create distance, perspective, and to take a philosophical tone. You can move sideways to transition from one idea to another, or just to expose yourself (see Chapter 5) to a larger section of the audience if the room and the crowd are large. The key to appropriate movement is somewhat paradoxical: it must be thoughtful and meaningful (unlike weight-shifting), but must also seem effortless and unrehearsed. Obviously, the only way to achieve this paradoxical combination is by doing it, often, in front of an audience. Like dancing, natural movement looks effortless when done well, and stiff and awkward when done badly. Also like dancing, an ideal rehearsal space would have a full-mirrored wall. Unfortunately, architects and designers seldom have access to a dance studio in which to rehearse their presentations. Until you get into the swing of things, plan your movement to relate to specific points of your discussion. When you become more experienced with moving in front of an audience, you can do less planning and trust your instincts to move at the right times (and stand still at the other times). For a graphic illustration of appropriate movement (albeit in an exaggerated context), rent the classic movie musical *The Music Man* and watch Robert Preston's riveting sales pitch as Professor Harold Hill in the number "Trouble." Why not aspire to such a dynamic, engaging, charismatic performance in your own presentations? You probably don't need to climb a statue, but what would happen if you did?

Summing It Up

Showing up is much more than being physically present at your presentation. It involves all of the following skills, which can be practiced and mastered over time:

- *Physical preparation.* Being aware of your physical body, its natural tension, and using that tension against itself in isometric exercises.

- *Mental preparation.* Leaving issues unrelated to the task at hand outside the presentation room.

- *Stage presence.* The degree to which you powerfully inhabit your own body and the space you have available to work in.
- *Appropriate movement.* Your willingness to dance for clients and other audiences will spell the difference between highly persuasive presentations and the mere delivery of content.

What's My Motivation?

This question is one that all actors ask themselves as they prepare their treatment of a character. Motivation is the driving force behind the words an actor says. Motivation, in the context of presenting, is the overriding goal of your presentation—your objective, in other words. Without a motivation, an actor's reading of lines will be uninspired at best, painfully mechanical at worst. Likewise, without a goal behind your presentation, your delivery will be equally unremarkable.

Motivation for an actor is often the unstated goal of the character. It seldom is revealed in the dialogue itself. Likewise, for a presenter, your motivation is for you to know and your audience to discover. Your goal need not be stated explicitly in your presentation, although you might choose to do so if your presentation calls for particular candor. What's critical is that your motivation be clear to you, and to others presenting with you, and that everyone on your presentation team have the same goal in mind as the presentation is put together. While in a play, different characters may have wildly different motivations, in a presentation, you should be unified in your desire to persuade.

Persuasive or Informative?

In school, speech students are often taught that there are two (or more) types of speeches, the principal types being persuasive and informative. It is the strongly held opinion of the author that those two types should be relabeled as persuasive and boring. An informative speech in the design professions might be one entitled, "Uses for Recycled Wood Products in Construction." Does this sound like a speech you would want to attend? Like a speech anyone would want to attend?

A persuasive title for a talk on the latter topic might be "Recycled Wood Products: The Future of Casework." By making the title (and presumably also the talk) assertive instead of informative, the speaker has given him- or herself a goal—to persuade the audience of the inevitability of recycled wood products in interior casework. In so doing, the stage is set for a dynamic, challenging, and ultimately persuasive presentation. The original title (and corresponding talk), on the other hand, is devoted solely to the delivery of content, which the listener could just as easily learn by reading a paper on the subject. There is no point to making an informative presentation precisely because there is no point to an informative presentation.

Focus on the Objective

In order for your persuasive presentation to actually persuade anyone, you need to remain focused on

TIP

Every speech you give should have a persuasive goal. The alternative is to be informative—and boring.

What's My Motivation?

your objective. This can be more difficult than it sounds in a technical professional presentation, because such presentations are often filled with content that the audience has specifically asked you to address. This content, which is like the (long-lost) "compulsory" figures in figure skating, is inherently less interesting than the part of your presentation where you really get to focus on your most persuasive points. The challenge for the design professional is to figure out how to get through the compulsories while staying focused on the overall objective of the presentation.

A clarifying thought is in order here. A presentation can have many points, subpoints, and counterpoints, but it can have only one objective. Sometimes architects confuse content with the objective, thinking, for example, that the objective is to convey their relevant experience, the qualifications of their key staff, and their approach to the project. Clearly, if those were the objectives, there would be three of them, unrelated and almost irrelevant to each other. The latter items might be key components of the presentation, but none of them is the objective. Obviously, in the above example, the objective is to win a commission.

REMINDER

A presentation can have many points, subpoints, and counterpoints, but it can have only one objective.

It may seem overly obvious and unnecessary to point out, but this objective, simple as it is, should inform every aspect of the presentation, including the previously mentioned key chunks of content. A simple way to do this is to apply a test to every content point in the presentation: Is this point necessary to achieve our objective? Second, if it is necessary, does it effectively communicate something that will bring the objective closer to being met? Again, it may seem overly obvious to the reader, but the shocking fact is that architects and designers hurt themselves most often in presentations by their failure to apply this simple test. Presentations in which architects dwell endlessly on the beauty and brilliance of their past work is a case in point. While everyone enjoys seeing pretty photographs of completed projects, a presenter must challenge him- or herself, to determine whether showing this work does anything to move the audience toward the goal (again, in this instance, the assumed goal is gaining a commission). It shouldn't take you long to think of the last presentation you saw by an architect or designer where a great deal of extraneous information was presented, which seemed to be more for the speaker's enjoyment than anyone else's. Perhaps that unfortunate speaker was you.

Staying focused on the objective will help you shorten, tighten, focus, and generally improve your presentations as much as any other technique that is

But I Really Want to Say This!

One of the most difficult distinctions a presenter has to make is between what you want to say and what the audience needs to hear. The objective test—will it help you meet your objective?—is the best guide to whether to include content or leave it out. Rationalizations design professionals sometimes use for including extraneous content include:

▶ "It may not be important to them, but it's important to me." Too obvious to require a response.

▶ "We may lose points if we don't cover this." It's good to respond to issues you know you'll be scored on. But if you don't know what those issues are, you shouldn't assume you do.

▶ "They really need to hear this!" This is where the presenter turns into a preacher, and the audience into sinners in need of saving.

▶ "They didn't ask for it, but they should have." Once again puts you in the position of deciding what's important to the audience.

What's My Motivation?

presented in this book. In fact, if you fail to stay focused on your objective, all the other techniques mentioned in this book will be of minimal value in helping you gain your ultimate goal, whatever that might be. Use a clear statement of your objective (to yourself and those on your team) to serve as an unforgiving editor, slashing and burning unnecessary information, self-congratulatory words, and extraneous points, until your presentation is tightly wrapped around a single, compelling idea.

An objection may be made that, as noted above, sometimes clients require information to be presented that, in some sense, is unrelated to the objective of the presentation. The challenge in cases like this is to make the required information fit the objective, either in its form or its presentation. For example, if a client specifically asks for a recitation of past work, you can make the recitation as brief or as perfunctory as will meet the requirement and not

A Moment of Clarity

What are some examples of clear objectives for a talk?

► I want to convince the audience that they should only use low-emissivity glass in every project they build from now on.

► I want the audience to be so engaged in the discussion that they forget to bring in the next presenter.

► I want the audience to understand our design philosophy so well that they could repeat it to a stranger tomorrow.

► I want the audience to believe with all their hearts that we are qualified for this project, even though we haven't done ten others like it.

► I want the commission to approve this design with few or no modifications.

It shouldn't need to be pointed out that one, and only one, of the above examples could be the motivation for a presentation. If you have multiple objectives, you will reduce your chances of reaching any of them.

detract from your larger goal. This approach is more likely to be successful than viewing the above requirement as an invitation to survey your career.

The Story Line

In order to meet your objective for a presentation, it is helpful to hang the presentation on a narrative idea. This idea, which might be called a story line, is another way to distinguish your talk from the mere delivery of content, or the dreaded informative speech.

As an example of story line, think about ABC's *Monday Night Football*. When the announcers are building up the game, they don't say things like, "The Miami Dolphins are facing a must-win situation tonight against division rival Baltimore Ravens." This statement might be factually accurate, and might describe the status of the Miami Dolphins fairly well, but it is not a story line. The story line goes more like this: "It's crunch time for the Dolphins, and the question head coach Jimmy Johnson has to answer is this: Does aging quarterback Dan Marino still have what it takes to bring a Super Bowl trophy to Miami?"

Do you see the differences? One difference is in the use of language: the story line uses dynamic words and phrases as opposed to bland statements of fact. This aspect of the story line deals with the emotional content of the contest being promoted. Another notable difference between the two accounts is that the second one is highly personalized—it's not about the Miami Dolphins; it's about "head coach Jimmy Johnson" and "aging quarterback Dan Marino." By making the story personal, it is invested with much greater intensity and meaning than the dry account of the standings in the AFC East Division.

Philosopher David Hume theorized that what makes something memorable is the intensity and vivacity of the impression it makes on us. Intensity is fairly easy to understand—this is why fireworks are memorable and sparklers are not. Vivacity is a little more difficult: vivacious means "full of life," or lively. All presenters are presumably alive. What makes one presentation more lively than another? It is the story line that humanizes a presentation and makes it vivacious.

Here's another illustration, one perhaps less remote than NFL Football. Suppose you were invited to attend a presentation on lighting products: The lights dim, the speaker rises and says, "There are four principal lamp types commonly in use in North America, each of which has advantages and disadvantages." What the speaker has begun is factual, true, and presumably important to your professional advancement. Are you engaged? Are you dying to hear what comes next?

Now suppose, at the same seminar, the lights dim and the same speaker gets up and says, "Ellen Herkmeyer has a serious problem. She's the facility manager for ACME Toolco, a high-tech manufacturer of machine parts. Her boss, the VP of operations, has just given Ellen the task of cutting facility operations costs by 15 percent in the next six months. Do you know what Ellen should do? What would you do?" This speaker is about to give you the same information about types of lighting devices that the first speaker did. It may take a little longer to get to the four basic types of lamps, but when you do get there, will you be more or less engaged than in the previous example? Do you know Ellen Herkmeyer? Probably not. But by personalizing the talk, by giving it a story line (which can presumably be developed during the course of the talk to show how an understanding of lamp types led to Ellen meeting her boss's goal), you have (most likely) been drawn into the discussion, given a reason to care, and become emotionally invested in the outcome.

If you think about it, this is the reason why people pay money to see movies, but can't be paid to sit through a slide show of someone else's vacation. Even a good vacation photographer will fail to draw an audience if there is no emotional content in the presentation. Which brings up a point about what a story line is not: it is not a story line if you have a chronological narrative (i.e., "my Paris vacation: here we are at the airport leaving for Paris") devoid of any conflict, tension, or problem needing to be solved. Remember Professor Harold Hill: when faced with the fact that nothing much was troubling the little town of River City, Iowa, he decides he'll have to invent some trouble—and uses the mayor's billiard parlor as the source of all the town's presumed troubles. This is not to suggest that you manufacture problems where they don't really exist, but that you search for the dramatic component—the tension, the anxiety, the conflict—that animates the problem you are trying to solve with yourself, your firm, or your design as the proposed solution.

For a story line to make sense, it has to have two key elements: plot and characters. Setting, a third element, may be necessary for fiction, but is not as essential to a presentation story line. Characters are the "who" of the story. Your audience will be more interested in your presentation if people are involved in the story.

Plot is the "what," as in, "What happened to Ellen Herkmeyer? Did she meet her goal of cutting operating costs?" Plot suggests the progression of a story from introducing the characters, establishing what their predicament is, and then showing how the characters or some other element helps to resolve the conflict. If you can figure out the plot of your own presentation, you will have a much more compelling story to tell than if you stand up and begin to recite your qualifications.

Presentation Formats

Presentations take place in a wide variety of settings, ranging from the extremely formal (the delivery of a scientific paper, for instance) to the extremely informal (telling a new acquaintance what your firm does at a golf outing or a cocktail party). There is a degree of preparation involved that corresponds to the formality or informality of the setting, as well. In this section, we'll look at different presentation formats and how they relate to your ability to foster interaction, a key to successful presenting.

In general, the more you are able to interact with your audience, whatever the size of that audience, the more successful your presentation is likely to be. Interaction bridges the gap between speaker and audience, and allows you to connect with them as individuals, so that you become less of a "show" and more of a real person to your listeners. To continue the metaphor from the previous chapter, in interacting with your audience, you invite them to join the dance.

TIP
The more you are able to interact with your audience, whatever the size, the more successful your presentation is likely to be.

Many architects and designers are fearful of interacting with an audience (especially a selection committee). Objections they raise include such concerns as, "What if I ask them a question and nobody says anything?" or, "Selection committees want to judge my performance. They don't want to be a part of it."

These objections, while quite common, are not borne out by experience. Rare indeed is the selection committee that does not value and enjoy having its opinions solicited directly by a presenter. The "presentation followed by questions and answers" format of most marketing interviews is a defensive measure adopted by clients to ensure that you don't monopolize the entire time of the interview with your prepared remarks. Few architects consider the other alternative: an interview consisting entirely of questions and answers, including some questions asked of the committee by the presenter. This approach actually has a higher probability of success than one in which a formal presentation proceeds without interruption for the allotted time period. It engages the audience in a discussion, making it possible to interact over issues of significance, as opposed to the formal stating of positions that characterizes a presentation without interruption.

"People will give mental and verbal assent to what you tell them, but will believe with conviction what they discover for themselves."
—RICK WARREN
The Purpose-Driven Church

The importance of interaction is impossible to overstate. How interaction relates to presentation formats is that, to the extent that you are able to influence the format, you should always choose a

What's My Motivation?

presentation format that allows for the most interaction (see Figure 2.1). This is true regardless of the size of the audience. Many presenters mistakenly assume that interaction declines rapidly as audience size increases. In a simplified formula, you can see that interaction necessarily decreases as audience size increases. But critically, it doesn't (or shouldn't) decrease in direct proportion (see Figure 2.2). If your audience has twenty people in it there will be slightly less interaction than if it has ten—but not half as much. Likewise, if your audience is two hundred, there shouldn't be 95 percent less interaction than if there were only ten listeners. Your goal, regardless of audience size, should be to interact with them as much as possible. This is one of the ways you will create empathy between you and your listeners, a

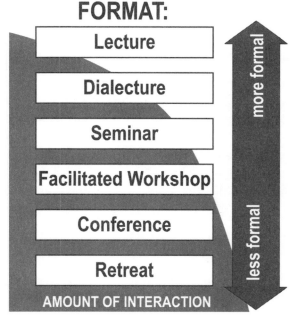

Figure 2.1

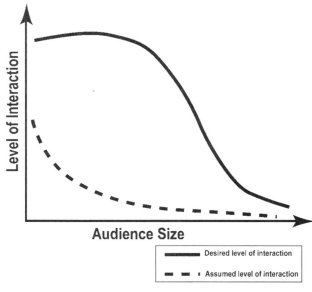

Figure 2.2

topic that will be looked at more extensively in Chapter 5.

There are several formats a presentation could take. Following is a list of several common formats, together with a brief discussion of each. They are arranged in order from most to least formal, with the strong implication that to the degree you have any say in the matter, you should move your discussion toward the informal end of the scale, the better to promote interaction.

Lecture

In a lecture, one or more speakers are parked at a podium (with or without visual aids), spewing content at an entirely passive audience. This is the "I talk, you listen" format for dispensing knowledge—and a purely intellectual activity. Because of the passivity

A Quick Look at Formats

► *Lecture:* The proverbial "talking head," with content delivered from Mount Olympus.

► *Dialecture*: Content delivery with planned interaction.

► *Seminar:* More open discussion with a knowledgeable leader.

► *Facilitated Workshop:* Open discussion with a nonknowledgeable leader who can facilitate.

► *Conference:* Discussion with informal leadership.

► *Retreat:* Wide-open discussion, sometimes lacking even a topic.

of the audience, and the general lack of movement on the part of the speaker, lectures are the most formal, least engaging type of presentation. Speakers who are themselves engaging (Billy Graham, for example) can pull off this format better than amateurs. For a design professional to embrace the lecture format requires either a commitment to battle against its strictures (for example, moving out from behind the lectern) or a willingness to bore your audience, as many college professors do.

Dialecture

The term "dialecture" is a neologism coined by theologian Dr. John Gerstner for his favorite way of presenting information: a presentation involving one or more speakers in front of a chalkboard spewing content, with a key difference: the speaker welcomes, even encourages, interaction with the group. Dialecture allows for clarification and questions and, therefore, greatly improves the chances that the content will sink in. The key to making dialecture work is the willingness of the speaker to stem the flow of ideas long enough for one of the hearers to ask a question. This can be difficult if you speak like a human fire hydrant, blasting out ideas at high velocity without pause. But done correctly, the dialecture is one of the most effective "one-on-many" formats for speaking.

Seminar

In the seminar format, a leader, presumably with greater knowledge of the subject, leads a discussion of an idea or topic. Others in attendance are expected to participate, although there is a parallel expectation that the leader will say more (and have more to say) than most of the participants. Seminars allow all participants an opportunity to contribute to understanding of the topic—both their own and the understanding of others. A limitation of seminars is group size: with more than about twenty or so participants, the level of group participation becomes diminished and less meaningful. For most design-related presentations, however, the seminar format is a good fit.

Facilitated Workshop

The facilitated workshop looks a lot like a seminar and may take place in the same room arrangement. There is one key difference, however. In the facilitated workshop, a leader, not necessarily with greater or specialized knowledge, helps a group discuss an idea or problem in an orderly fashion. The key difference is that the leader (i.e., you) may not know as much about the subject as the participants. This format is an excellent choice when you don't possess mastery of the topic (see Chapter 3) or you need more information about the problem. The collaborative format and humble role of the facilitator is helpful in establishing a sense of collaboration

What's My Motivation?

among those present. This format works especially well for architects because we so seldom know more about our clients' business than they do.

Conference

A conference, not surprisingly, is a gathering of peers with different perspectives, meeting to discuss a problem or topic. (This format is not to be confused with a "conference" presentation, which is a large gathering of colleagues from diverse regions meeting to discuss a problem or topic in a conference or convention center. This type of "conference" tends to favor lecture presentations, although less formal settings are both possible and desirable). Conference presentations are often leaderless, or a leader is self-selected by reason of position or personality. From a presenter's point of view, a conference should be a "sit-down" presentation, that is, one where very little "presenting" gets done. The more casual the setting, the more likely you are to achieve your objective.

Retreat

In this least formal arrangement, a group of peers gather to discuss one or more topics with great informality, often no direction, and sometimes no targeted outcomes. One might argue that a retreat setting is so informal that your objective (see discussion of motivation above) becomes unattainable. But the retreat setting is one in which the interaction around an idea can be most effective, because pressures of time and the formality of normal business can be put aside. Viewed in this way, the informality of a retreat can be a great setting for presenting, provided you are prepared and that your presentation doesn't violate the spirit of informality (a computerized overhead presentation might not be the best technology for the setting). Because active participation is expected, ideas at retreats are often developed on the spot by means of brainstorming and interaction.

Choosing a Format

The choice of which format to use—again, assuming you have a choice—should be based on the answer to the question "What's my motivation?" What are you trying to get your hearers to do? It should be obvious, although many architects miss this point: lecturing an audience may impress them with your encyclopedic knowledge, but it will not likely persuade them that you are a stimulating person to work with. As you look over the range of options from lecture to retreat, notice that the status of the speaker relative to the other participants is reduced as the format becomes more informal. This fact ties directly to the believability of your own claims about collaboration, interaction, and teamwork. The lecturer lecturing about collaboration is likely to be viewed by his or her audience as a self-important show-off, rather than a real collaborator.

How to Talk

Another fundamental aspect of speaking, related to finding your motivation, is deciding how you will speak. This decision is not as obvious as it sounds. Of course, unless you're presenting abroad, you will speak in English, and out loud, as opposed to telepathically. But there are several ways to talk, and, as with the choice of format, the method you choose will have some bearing on your ultimate success in reaching your objective.

A Quick Look at How to Talk

- ► *Memorize your talk,* if you have been to acting school, have the time to do it, and are confident that you won't mess up.
- ► *Speak from a manuscript,* if you're testifying before Congress. Otherwise, avoid at all costs.
- ► *Speak from an outline,* to help you stay organized but to give fresh expression to each idea.
- ► *Speak extemporaneously,* to demonstrate your mastery of the topic.
- ► *Speak improvisationally,* to demonstrate your creativity and openness to sudden flashes of inspiration.

The following discussion will outline several of the various ways you can deliver an oral presentation, apart from the format of the presentation itself. This range of options has more to do with how you speak than with how you interact with your audience. As with presentation formats, however, the choices range from more to less formal (see Figure 2.3).

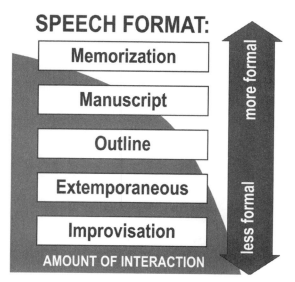

Figure 2.3

Memorization

The most formal way to deliver a talk is to memorize a manuscript from start to finish. While this method has the advantage of ensuring that you'll say exactly what you wanted to say the day before the presentation, several disadvantages come to mind. First, memorization is hard work for most people, and it becomes harder as they get older. An eight-minute speech requires four to five pages of double-spaced typing, which would be a tall order for a professional actor, let alone a busy design professional. Actors have the added advantage—usually—of another actor to play off of, which helps reduce the likelihood of the second problem: forgetting your lines. Memorization is the high-wire act of public speaking, because if you stumble, there is no safety net. Worse, memorized speeches can (and often do) sound canned unless you are gifted in the skill of bringing emotional nuance to each idea you bring up. Professional actors struggle with keeping a role fresh—how much more will an overworked design professional struggle with keeping a memorized speech fresh!

WARNING

Memorizing a speech is likely to lead to a stilted and boring presentation—unless you are a professional actor.

Manuscript

While memorization is clearly not the best option for most speakers, many are tempted to read from a manuscript. This may be the single worst way to convey information orally. Reading a manuscript insults the audience by conveying only what the audience could gain by reading for themselves. (One might make exception for a poetry reading or an author reading his or her own novel, but these are literary events, not persuasive presentations. Another exception might be the presentation of a scholarly

What's My Motivation?

An Actor Looks at Memorization

One argument that is made in favor of memorizing speeches is, "Isn't that what real performers do? Aren't all their speeches memorized?" Of course, professional (and amateur) actors memorize their lines. What makes them professional actors (and what differentiates them from amateur actors) is the ability to deliver memorized lines in a way that doesn't *sound* memorized. Amateur actors often fall into a singsong delivery that is inappropriately poetic because the rhythm of the language helped them memorize a speech. But that rhythm often sounds strange to an audience.

Another aspect of memorization is the problem of soliloquies. Actors generally fear long soliloquies, which are solo speeches that run on for a page or more of the script, because they are, frankly, more difficult to memorize than dialog. In a dialog, you only have to remember half the conversation word for word, and your fellow actors are continually providing you contextual clues as to what your next line should be. Good actors are so comfortable with dialog that they can improvise on the spot when another actor "goes up" (forgets his or her lines). With soliloquies, the actor is alone on stage, with no one to help out if his or her brain seizes up. That is why soliloquies are the bane of most professional actors.

The implications for architects are obvious, or should be. Don't assign yourself—or anyone else—speeches that run on for countless minutes. (To an actor, a two-minute soliloquy is a "long" speech.) Break up discussions of technical topics; have multiple speakers provide input, to combat boredom and reduce the chances of someone "going up." One reason that playwrights use soliloquies sparingly, if at all, is the risk of boring the audience with a single speaker for very long. Why shouldn't design professionals use the same cautious judgment in preparing presentations?

paper where the author is constrained by custom to read his or her manuscript; but, again, this is more an academic ritual than a professional practice.) In the real world, where designers practice, reading from a manuscript is a guaranteed ticket to a bored and indifferent audience, and to the almost certain failure of reaching your objective for the presentation. Like memorization, its lone advantage is that you will say only the words you intended, but this advantage is trifling compared to the suffering you will inflict on your audience.

Outline

Vastly preferable to speaking from a manuscript is speaking from an outline. An outline can help keep you organized and on the subject, but without the deadly monotony of reading from a script. We all learned to create outlines in school (we did, didn't we?), and their structure is not as important as the structure of the argument you are outlining. It doesn't really matter if you prefer Roman numerals or A-B-C, if you indent your subpoints, or if your outline is on an index card or a projection screen. What matters in speaking from an outline is that you use brief fragments of ideas to jog your memory of what to speak about, using language that is fresh each time you say it. Of particular importance is that the language you use not be the exact wording of your outline, in which case you find yourself reading from a very brief, telegraphic, and, at times, incomprehensible script. More will be said about the proper uses of computer presentation software in the appendix; at this point, it is sufficient to note that most presentations that use computerized overheads are in fact outline presentations.

Extemporaneous

Of the methods listed here, this is the one most likely to achieve your objective for your presentation. The word "extemporaneous" comes from the Latin phrase *ex tempore*, or "at the moment." What it means is saying words that come to you at the time you are speaking. Unlike with the next method of talking, however, extemporaneous speaking is not made up from nothing, like a whimsical story. To speak extemporaneously requires a great deal of preparation and thorough knowledge of the subject at hand. In that way, it is like memorization, with one crucial difference: in memorization, the focus is on the particular words to be conveyed, on preserving exactly their order and structure as it was first written down. In extemporaneous speaking, the focus is not on the particular words, but on the ideas that are to be conveyed. The extemporaneous speaker believes and trusts that if the ideas are well understood and the argument well crafted, the right words will follow easily.

It is the author's experience that the most persuasive speakers in any context speak extemporaneously, where their obvious command of the subject matter conveys on them an authority and trustworthiness that even the best-crafted script cannot. It is in speaking extemporaneously about a subject, with obvious passion, keen interest, and deep experience, that a speaker can most easily and effectively persuade his or her audience to assent to his or her primary objective. Extemporaneous presenting is the dance that the audience wants to see.

At the practical level, speaking *ex tempore* means that you do not use any notes at all. If there are visual aids related to your talk, they do not contain the key points of your discussion (or if they do, you do not follow them; they seem to follow you). It means you are free to move around the space you have at your disposal, to gesture and to engage the audience in a variety of ways. Most important, it means you are able to address questions or comments that come from the audience without feeling as if you have

The Blank Agenda

One method of presenting that is both daring and potentially rewarding exists in the twilight zone between extemporaneous and improvisational speaking. That is the "blank agenda" presentation. In this method, as the presentation is about to begin, the lead presenter asks the audience which topics should be covered during the presentation. The topics are written on a flip chart or whiteboard, and then the presentation follows the agenda as determined by the audience, rather than by the presenters. While this may sound wildly dangerous, it's not as difficult as it might appear at first glance. It does require careful advance preparation, as any good improviser will know.

The key to the blank agenda is your ability to anticipate which major points of discussion the audience is likely to ask for, and to have prepared specific segments addressing those points. In this way, the only unknown is the order in which your presentation will be given. If your client wants to talk about the budget first, fine, talk about the budget first. You simply need to have all the possible areas of discussion assigned to a person or persons, and then lead your team through them in the sequence set by the audience. It's not as difficult as it sounds, and it makes your team look amazingly responsive and light on their feet. Plus, it makes the audience feel as if they have a real role in the presentation, rather than being passive victims of it.

been thrown for a loop (this idea is developed more fully in Chapter 8).

Improvisation

As anyone familiar with the comedic form of theater known popularly as "improv" knows, improvisation means making it up as you go along. While this technique is daring and can be spectacular if done well, the risk of failure is too great to recommend it. To approach a presentation as an improvisation means to react only to the stimulus of the moment: the questions or comments of the audience, the visuals you create at the time of the presentation, the ideas of your colleagues. Potentially, an improvised presentation can be a masterful work of performance art, as viewers of the television program *Whose Line Is It Anyway?* may recall. At its worst, however, an improvised presentation makes you look unprepared, lackadaisical, disinterested, and unprofessional. These risks are substantial in even the most low-level presentation and tend to militate against improvisation as a speaking method.

RULE OF THUMB

The risk of failure is too great to recommend improvisation as a method of speaking for design professionals.

One interesting insight to the discussion of improv from the world of show business is the realization of how little of improvisation is actually improvised. Comedy groups that specialize in improv

Salty Language

*"You can lead a horse to water,
but if you put salt in his oats,
you can be sure he'll drink."*
—Gary Smalley

Obviously, using profanity (salty language) to spice up a presentation is ill-advised. But author and speaker Gary Smalley advises speakers to "salt" their conversation with highlights of coming attractions to retain the listener's interest. The "salt" is simply a hint of something interesting that's coming up later (e.g., "We have some exciting ideas to show you, which we'll get to in a few minutes."). This is analogous to what local newscasts do every day, when they tease you with stories that are scheduled to be shown in the waning minutes of the broadcast, just to keep you tuned in.

How do you salt a presentation effectively? Here are some tips:

► Allude to something without actually naming it.

► Reveal the structure of the presentation to the audience, so they know what to expect, and in what order.

► Keep the audience aware of where you are in your presentation.

► Defer answers to questions ("Great question—we plan to cover that in just a minute, if you'll bear with us.").

► Save something important for the end of the presentation—don't use your best "story" (to use the news metaphor) up front.

are loathe to admit it, but much of what passes for brilliant spur-of-the-moment comedy is in fact material that has been prepared in advance, or at least answers to questions that have been asked many times before. An experienced improviser has a whole repertoire of canned "bits" that can be pressed into service in almost any situation—a good strategy to employ should you be inclined to risk the art of improvisation.

Summing It Up

The effective presentation depends on the speaker having a clear objective in mind. This objective can be thought of as the speaker's motivation for everything that is said in a presentation. Some important attributes of understanding your motivation and making the most of it in a talk are:

- ► Defining the single objective of your talk as a goal to be achieved or an action you want the audience to take as a result of your talk (e.g., "Hire us.").

- ► Shaping your talk around a story line, a simple narrative idea that gives it a plot and character, making it personal rather than merely a recitation of facts.

- ► Choosing (to the extent you have a choice) a presentation format that achieves the highest possible level of interaction with your audience.

- ► Choosing a method of speaking that will help you achieve your objective. In the author's opinion, extemporaneous speaking is the method most likely to do this, with speaking from an outline a close second.

Know Your Lines

3

"*The successful performer is not the person with the truth, but the one with the sharpest tongue and the handiest numbers.*"
—MARK KINGWELL
University of Toronto

The quintessential actor's nightmare is one in which you find yourself thrust onto a stage in a play you are unfamiliar with, with other actors delivering their lines and looking at your expectantly. The problem is, you haven't even so much as read the script, and have no idea what your lines are.

Knowing your lines, a fundamental rule of the theater, may seem an odd commandment in a discussion of professional presentations, particularly in light of the discussion in the previous chapter about the undesirability of memorization. But knowing your lines in the context of professional presentations is something rather different from an actor's need to memorize his or her portion of a script. Knowing your lines has more to do with the preparation required to accomplish your presentation's goal.

The Key to Successful Presentations

"Fortune favors the prepared mind."
—PETER DRUCKER

If there is a single key that opens the door to successful presentations, it is not a trick of technique, or the ability to remember names, or the winning smile. It is simply this one thing: mastery of the topic. If you think back to the most successful speeches or talks you have ever heard, in any forum, you will be compelled to agree that what all these successful speakers had in common was that they knew what they were talking about. Or at least they seemed to.

Mastery of the topic is a simple idea that is complex in application, and it contains many facets that need to be explored. But at the core of the commandment to "know your lines" is the recognition that any successful presenter must be in control of the content, in possession of the salient facts, and have enough knowledge of the subject to be both interesting and compelling to the audience.

So what does mastery of the topic look like? It might look like an evangelist giving a message on a book of the Bible, or a comedian working an audience with a routine that has been crafted in countless clubs in innumerable towns across the nation. It might look like a pilot briefing a tour group on the capabilities of the aircraft he or she flies, or a product demonstration in a shopping center. But in each case, the persuasiveness and authority of the presenter is tied to his or her mastery of the topic being discussed. This is actually much more important than whether or not the speaker has an accent, or brown shoes, or lipstick on her teeth. A true master, whether an architect or a cobbler, will be a compelling speaker despite the superficial defects in appearance or speech that speakers tend to obsess about.

Conversely, think about ineffective speakers you may have heard. In most cases, the root of their ineffectiveness was probably not an annoying personal habit, such as jingling car keys (as bad as that is); more likely it was the underlying nervousness that habit betrayed. Underlying nervousness caused not so much by stage fright as by a subject that was not fully in the speaker's grasp, an elusive butterfly of an idea that no amount of jingling could pin down because the speaker had not mastered the topic to begin with.

Let's examine the ingredients that make mastery of the topic possible for a design professional. The key elements to mastering a topic are research and rehearsal. But as you will see, rehearsal is not the kind of practice one normally thinks of in preparing a speech. There are two critical aspects to a presentation: the content and the delivery. But while preparing content may be fairly straightforward, preparing the delivery is not as dependent on repetition as it is on broad experience. First, let's look at the content side of the equation.

RULE OF THUMB

If there is a single key that opens the door to successful presentations, it is mastery of the topic.

Research

It's not really that hard to win a debate tournament—all it takes is a whole lot of work. The successful debater is the person who has out-researched his or her opponent and is able to call that research to mind in the pressurized setting of the debate. This is true for a couple of reasons. First, the debater who is better prepared knows he or she is better prepared, and this knowledge helps to produce confidence and relaxation. Second, the judges of the debate (the audience) recognize and respect the superior effort of the debater who is better prepared. One might go so far as to say that facts themselves garner points for the debater, almost without respect to their relevance, or even to their accuracy. In North America at least, the bolstering of an argument by facts seems to outweigh other considerations of logic or eloquence.

It might be objected, and quite correctly, that professional presentations are not debating tournaments. But a persuasive presentation, even in a noncompetitive (i.e., not a sales) setting, is really a debate tournament with an invisible opponent: to mix metaphors, it is debate shadow-boxing. Your opponent is the audience's skepticism, hesitancy, and unwillingness to undertake what you are trying to get them to think or do. This opponent is more formidable than a debating counterpart, because their defenses are mostly passive, and you have little information to react to as you are building your case.

REMINDER

Your opponent is the audience's skepticism, hesitancy, and unwillingness to undertake what you are trying to get them to think or do.

But building a case is exactly what you are doing. And research is the key to doing it effectively. So often design professionals try to skate through presentations on their own charm and talent, or perhaps on the obvious appeal of the drawings or other visuals that they have in tow. In fact, every presentation should be viewed as a trial, with a skeptical jury waiting to be convinced beyond a reasonable doubt of the validity of your position. As debates demand facts, so trials demand evidence. And it is the weight of this evidence, rather than your rhetorical skill, that will work to accomplish your objective. Is it possible that too many design professionals rely on their brilliant salesmanship to carry the day, when they should be spending more time in preparation and research?

Know Your Lines

Facts and Factoids

"There is nothing like instances to grow hair on a bald-headed argument."
—MARK TWAIN

One of the most persuasive building blocks of a compelling argument is factual information. In our society, nothing says "fact" like numbers. So rather than saying, "Our firm has designed several outstanding fire stations," you might say, "Our firm has designed eight fire stations very similar to this one." Or, instead of saying, "We are very attentive to cost control," you might say, "Our firm has completed 24 of our last 26 projects within budget, and the two that weren't, were only over by an average of 2.5 percent." Do you see how much more compelling, in both instances, the second statement is than the first? This assumes, of course, that the facts you are spouting happen to be true. You may get away with fabricated facts for a brief time, but eventually the fabrications will catch up to you, to disastrous effect.

RULE OF THUMB

In our society, nothing says "fact" like numbers.

Factoids are like facts, but, like the *USA Today* newspaper, are more easily digested. Factoids are good for demonstrating a command of your subject. Again, compare the statement, "We have a lot of experience designing schools" with the statement, "A recent congressional survey showed that three out of four American schoolchildren attend a building with substandard conditions." Even though the second statement is not about your firm at all, it creates a stronger support for your argument than the bland generalization "We know a lot about schools."

The key benefit of facts and factoids is their specificity. This specificity requires that you do some research (How many schools are there in your community? What percentage of them are substandard?). And it is this specific knowledge of facts, facts that you have available at your command, that makes you a master of your topic and a more believable presenter.

An objection might be raised at this point: If memorization is bad, how does one present facts and factoids without memorizing them? There are a couple of responses. First, it is good to memorize facts, but not the words you put around those facts in a presentation context. If memorization of facts is difficult, there is no harm in using notes to give you a feeling of security. But if you end up reading your notes to the audience, whether from a pad, note card, or a projected image, your facts may still carry some weight, but you will lose much of your credibility as a master of the topic. You don't have to have every fact memorized, but you have to be familiar enough with each fact so that it rolls off your tongue as matter-of-factly as if you had just asked someone to pass the salt.

A master debater, Bill Clinton, at the time, governor of Arkansas, dramatically demonstrated the value of facts and factoids during his campaign debates with then-President George Bush. President Bush said that he was in favor of protecting Social Security. Clinton gave lengthy and detailed answers showing that he knew not only that Social Security was in trouble, but the year it would run out of funds and how we should go about fixing it. The fact that Social Security had not been reformed after eight years of Clinton's presidency is beside the point— the point is that the superior debater won the debates (and the election) with his powerful command of the facts.

Rehearsal

Mastery of the topic through intense preparation is one-half of the secret to knowing your lines. The other half is the ability—and the confidence—to deliver the material you have prepared in a compelling manner. To most designers, this means rehearsing a presentation. And, since most architects don't know any better, they often rehearse by going over what they plan to say in excruciating detail, reading from a manuscript until the words become imprinted on their brain. This is not the method that will be recommended here.

Far worse than rote rehearsal, however, is the sin of not rehearsing at all. For every bad presentation that has been over-rehearsed to the point of tedium, there is a worse presentation that has had no practice run whatsoever. Again, it is supreme arrogance on the part of design professionals to think that, because we are successful architects, or because we are busy, or because we think our time too valuable, we can breeze into a presentation, set up the easels, and accomplish the objective with our winsome smile and our sharply pressed suit. Even the simplest presentation requires you to be familiar with the components of the meeting: your agenda, your objective, your visual aids, the layout of the space, lighting, and so forth. To assume that everything will be where you need it when you need it is to set yourself up to fail spectacularly. So don't infer from the following that rehearsing is a no-no. We'll look shortly at how to practice in a way that makes achieving your presentation goal more likely.

The Practice Paradox

Unlike in the theater, where repetition is the key to solid memorization, professional presentations generally get worse the more they are repeated. Hence the Practice Paradox: You can practice speaking, but you can't (or shouldn't) practice a speech.

What does this mean? It means that going over the particular words of your presentation will tend to make you stiff and stale; and, paradoxically, the more you go over them, the more stiff and stale you will become. On the other hand, the more experience you have speaking in front of groups, the more confident, fluid, and relaxed you will be for any particular presentation. This realization comes far too late for many practitioners, who only realize later in their careers that what they needed was not a better speechwriter, but more opportunities to practice speaking.

The opportunities for architects to speak in front of groups both large and small are boundless. A few suggestions are listed below:

- ► Your AIA chapter probably has a speakers bureau, a database of architects who have identified themselves as willing to speak about architecture or a particular aspect of the profession to clubs or societies in need of a program. Most communities have a huge need for content providers who can deliver an interesting talk. Consider these groups a low-risk way to hone your presentation skills, as well as to market yourself and your firm.

- ► There are one or more professional or trade associations related to the type of facility you design most often—you may already be a member or an allied member of such a group. These groups have innumerable conferences and conventions, and most are grateful to have willing content providers.

- If you have children, consider speaking to a class about a relevant topic; or volunteer to speak at a career day. You don't even have to have children to do this, but you will have to find a school if you don't.

- There's always Toastmasters. This is an organization that exists solely to help its members hone their public speaking skills.

- Think outside the box: volunteer to host a dinner, run an auction, introduce a program at your AIA chapter. (Introducing other speakers can be a great way for nonspeakers to overcome paralyzing stage fright—it's a very low-risk activity).

The point is not so much what you do, it's that you take advantage of every opportunity that presents itself to present yourself to a group. It's not so much about marketing—very few qualified leads come from a career-day presentation—as it is about gaining confidence working a room in front of a group of people who may or may not be interested in what you have to say—just like at work!

The 1,000 Percent Rule

> *"Getting ready is preparation by immersion, but only about 10 percent of what you get is used. If you have something ready, it'll come out in a natural way. You can't be waiting to bring it up."*
>
> —TIM McCARVER

The McCarver quotation captures the essence of knowing your lines for a design professional: having prepared well enough that you are able to leave unsaid 90 percent of what you might be able to say.

In simple mathematical terms, this means having 1,000 percent of your content ready to go. It is the 1,000 percent principle that gives speakers real mastery of a topic—and leaves audiences with the important sensation that there is plenty more where that came from.

What does it take to get to 1,000 percent? Obviously, it takes more than showing up at a presentation with a junior designer who has been working all night on a set of drawings you've never seen before. It means, perhaps, staying up with the designer, or at least coming in early enough to get familiar with the work in advance of the presentation. It means knowing ten ways your visual aids can let you down (because they have in the past), and how to overcome each of them. It means knowing the questions your audience is likely to ask before they ask them, before they even think of them, and having thought about what your answers might be. It means understanding how the banks of light switches work.

TIP

If you cannot be adequately prepared to make a presentation, find someone else who can—even if you don't think they're as strong a presenter.

You might say, "That's all well and good, but sometimes my work requires that I make a presentation when I cannot be as prepared as I should be. What do I do then?" The answer is simple: Don't make the presentation. If you don't have time to be 1,000 percent prepared, you don't have any business presenting at all. Consider introducing a subordinate who has actually worked on the matter and letting them present it under your wise and judicious guidance. Such a presentation is more likely to be successful (assuming the two of you share the same goal) than your presenting something you have obviously not seen before in your life.

Helpful Rehearsal

So what about this big presentation you have to give next week? Is it being suggested that you don't rehearse at all, that you rely on your experience of having hosted a dinner last month for the Boy Scouts? Well, no. Some type of rehearsal is necessary, just not the kind where you repeat the same words until they become a meaningless mantra.

So what does a useful rehearsal look like? You need to organize a rehearsal the same way you organize the presentation itself. Your focus should be on content, but not solely on content. The following checklist will help you organize a rehearsal that will be useful in achieving your presentation goal:

➤ Whom am I presenting to? Ideally, you should know the names of everyone in the audience, and have done some research to learn what their principal concerns (often called "hot buttons") are.

➤ Where is the presentation taking place? If at all possible, you or a designee should visit the room you're presenting in before your rehearsal, so you can create a reasonable map of how your talk will be set up.

➤ What is your objective? (See Chapter 2, "What's My Motivation?")

➤ How long do I have to talk? Is this timeframe rigidly constrained or somewhat flexible?

➤ What kinds of visual aids will be most useful? Ideally, this decision will be made well in advance of your rehearsal, and you will have all your props ready to practice with. In the real world, this is seldom the case.

- ➤ Who will be talking? Identify people with a key role in the presentation, and those who are mainly there to provide backup for questions.

- ➤ How will the content be structured? (See the following section, "Structure").

- ➤ What are the principal content points that each speaker needs to cover? Once identified, does the speaker have enough information to address the points in detail? Remember Tim Carver's dictum about 90 percent of what you have ready not being used. Does each speaker have 1,000 percent of what he or she needs to cover?

Structure

Inasmuch as presentation formats have already been discussed, it may seem redundant to bring up the subject of structure now. Here, however, this topic refers not to the format of the presentation (lecture versus seminar versus workshop, etc.), but to the particular order of the information you have to present. A little structure is not a bad thing—very few clients (or anyone else, for that matter) appreciate a rambling stroll through the contents of your brain, with no real idea where you're headed or when you might get there. People appreciate some idea of what's coming up—to give them this idea requires that you structure your presentation.

Keeping in mind that all content should be in support of your objective, you should structure your presentation to be both simple and memorable. How? By strictly limiting the number and complexity of your main points. For example, if your presen-

TIP
People appreciate some idea of what's coming up—to give them this idea requires that you structure your presentation.

tation is a marketing effort, you might limit the main points to: "A little about us" (your team) and "A lot about your project" (your approach). Under those major headings might be three or four subheadings (e.g., "Managing Costs"), but the outline should be so simple that your audience has little chance of getting lost.

Some presentations benefit from the sledgehammer of clarity. This tool is commonly called the "tell-them-what-you're-going-to-tell-them, tell-them, then-tell-them-what-you-told-them" approach. While it may seem simplistic and perhaps overly pedantic, it often helps an audience to understand a technical presentation when the main points are unveiled at the outset, developed in the core of the presentation, then restated at the conclusion. This method leaves little room for doubt about what the main points of the presentation were supposed to be. The converse approach, to simply begin your talk and let the audience guess where you're going, is good for drama but generally bad for technical presentations. Even dramatic presentations (or at least musicals) have program notes that give a general idea where the action takes place and how the story is structured.

If your presentation is a simple one (e.g., you're there to present a design concept), you may not need to use the sledgehammer approach to structure. It may be sufficient to say, "We're here to show you our progress on the design—let us walk you through the drawings, and then we can discuss what our next steps need to be." Unless you work at the Pentagon, you don't need a twelve-item agenda for such a simple presentation. But most presentations you give should include some idea of what the audience should expect.

Summing It Up

In this chapter, we looked at the importance of "knowing your lines," which, in the context of our discussion, is the need for you to master the topic you are presenting. Mastery of the topic can quite literally be said to be the difference between a good presentation and a poor one.

As part of the idea of mastering the topic, the following supporting ideas were introduced:

- ► *Research.* If mastery of the topic is the key to successful presenting, research is the key to mastering your topic. There is no substitute for becoming overfamiliar with the material you are to present, which will give you a command of the facts, which will help you achieve your presentation goal.

- ► *Rehearsal.* Almost as important as research is giving yourself (and your team) adequate time to practice. However, the wrong kind of practice, rote recitation of your "lines," can do more harm than good.

- ► *The Practice Paradox.* You can practice speaking, but you can't practice a speech. Your best bet is to get in front of an audience as often as you possibly can, preferably in low-risk situations.

- ► *The 1000 percent rule.* In order to gain mastery of the topic, you need to know more than you are able to say. This surplus inventory of 900 percent of unused information is in fact the basis for mastery of a topic—it's the well you draw from that gives you confidence as a presenter.

- ► *Helpful rehearsal.* Don't worry so much about what you are going to say as about how your presentation is going to be run: understand the space and the furnishings; work with your team members to assure smooth transitions; and, at the risk of repetition, know as much as you possibly can about what you are going to talk about.

▶ *Structure*. Except for the simplest presentations, it is wise to organize your talk into an easily understandable structure and communicate that structure to your audience right at the beginning of the presentation.

Find Your Light

You would never think of producing a play, a concert, or even a skit without consideration of how to light the stage so the audience can see the players. Yet, amazingly, many design professionals are content to present in near-total darkness for fear of washing out the intensity of their slides. This mistake is so common that it has become standard practice in both academic and professional settings. And, as will be discussed in this chapter, most rooms where presentations occur lack reasonable control for lighting so that a compromise can be reached.

One of the first things an actor must learn to do when taking the stage for the first time is to find his or her light. This is because, unlike ordinary room lighting, stage lighting is highly directional, tightly focused, and definitely not uniform. Sometimes an actor must fudge the director's original blocking (instructions on where to stand and how to move) in order to find his or her light. But it is essential to find it, because if the audience can't see you, they can't hear you either.

For actors, finding their light means moving around on the stage until they can be seen. For archi-

REMINDER
If the audience can't see you, they can't hear you, either.

Be Seen to Be Heard: Why Is That?

It is a show business axiom that actors need to be seen to be heard. On the other hand, design professionals have sat through numerous slide presentations where the lecturer was a disembodied voice. So why is it that the audience can't hear you if they can't see you?

One reason is that hearing is an imperfect art. Listeners routinely gather 40 percent or less of what is said to them. Seeing a speaker is an aid to retention.

Seeing also gives clues to context. A speaker's face, body language, and gestures all contribute to the context of a discussion. Absent light, this context doesn't exist.

Finally, light calls attention to the speaker in contrast to other things that might draw a listener's interest. Architects and designers often wrongly assume that 100 percent of the listener's attention should be focused on the slide. This is not the case. The speaker's point about the slide is as important as the image, or more so.

tects, this idea will be expanded to include the complete presentation environment.

Understanding the Location

Because design professionals tend to view presenting as an intellectual exercise, like sending e-mail, they tend not to spend much time thinking about the environment in which they are to present. But as has been discussed, presenting is very much a theatrical and physical activity, as much about the who and the where as it is about the what. Accordingly, it is worth a considerable amount of time and effort to consider the stage on which your presentation is to take place.

Regrettably, most professional presentations don't occur in custom-designed meeting rooms with multilevel lighting controls and sophisticated rear-screen video projection. If you do enough presentations, you will see every manner of shabby conference room, school cafeteria, made-over break room, and undersized executive office used for design presentations. And, unfortunately, more often than not, the designer will have no say in the matter. But in case you do have a say, don't overlook the obvious: If you know of a better room or space in which to present, and your audience is not greatly inconvenienced, by all means ask for it! The worst that can happen is that your request will be denied and you will have to use the space that was originally planned.

The Goldilocks Problem

Presentation rooms are often too small to give you an effective stage, and only occasionally too big. A room that is too big makes it difficult to develop intimacy with your audience (see Chapter 5), but on the whole is preferable to one that is too small. A cramped presentation room not only can make you and your audience hot and uncomfortable, but it doesn't allow space for the dance to occur (see Chapter 1). If you and your colleagues are pinned to the wall by furniture that takes up too much of the available floor space, see if you can't push a few chairs out into the hall to give yourself some room to move. You may have to stand for the entire presentation, but unless you prefer to sit for the whole time, having room to move is probably the best choice.

On the rare occasion when the room you are given is too large, the best choice (if you have a choice) is to "waste" the space behind the audience, moving their seats as close as possible to the "stage" where you will be presenting. Don't feel that because a room is big you should spread out the furniture to fill it up. It is far better to create an intimate corner for interaction than to try to present across a gulf of

TIP

It is far better to create an intimate corner for interaction than to try to present across a gulf of empty space.

empty space. The "thrust stage" is a device popular with many stage directors because it puts the actors out among the audience, breaking the artificial barrier created by the traditional proscenium arch. Think of your presentations as being given mostly on a thrust stage, with the audience wrapped tightly around your team, rather than as separated from you by a proscenium and orchestra pit.

You need to think about where your audience will be seated (if you have access to the room before they come in, a desirable condition), and position their chairs so that they will have the best view of you and of your exhibits. Your main focus, besides being seen and being able to move, should be on providing for the comfort and convenience of your audience. Don't make them step over wires or scoot sideways past your team members to reach their seats.

The Dracula Problem

In your presentation space, you also need to be aware of where daylight may be coming from. Far stronger than any artificial illumination, even small amounts of direct sunlight can ruin a projected image. First, find out whether there is any window treatment (blinds, shades, curtains) you can employ to darken the room. If there is, test it to see whether it makes the room too dark. Sometimes, cracks of sunlight can be worse than broad patches of daylight in a presentation room. If you are using one, you should place your projection screen where it can't "see" the windows, just as you would locate a computer screen in an office.

Another hazard of daylight emerges when you are presenting in front of a large window or row of windows. The strong daylight will make you appear as a silhouette to your audience, regardless of how good the ambient room lighting may be. The fix is to take care to position your team, or at least the person speaking, so that there are no large expanses of windows behind them. Daylight in a presentation room is not a bad thing in itself, but like everything else about your presentation, it needs to be managed.

The Advance Team

It should go without saying, but probably needs to be said, that you should make every effort to check out the physical characteristics of the room in which you are presenting well in advance of the presentation. Days ahead is preferable to hours ahead, which is still preferable to minutes ahead. But as a professional, one of the easiest ways to make a fool of yourself is to traipse into the presentation room three minutes before your scheduled start time with a projector or an armload of easels and boards and say, "Let's see, now, where shall we set up?" This approach is both unprofessional and unlikely to work.

As a presenter, it is your responsibility to check out the room ahead of time. Send an assistant to do it only as a last resort, because his or her impression may be inaccurate, incomplete, or overlook some important detail you should have known about. It is almost unthinkable for an actor to take the stage, even in a touring production of one-night shows, for the first time when the audience is already in the house. Such lack of preparation and foresight would be extremely unprofessional. Why should the design professionals treat their performance platform any differently?

In some unusual circumstances, you will not be given access to the presentation room until the

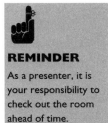

REMINDER

As a presenter, it is your responsibility to check out the room ahead of time.

Find Your Light

moment of your presentation. In this event, you need to make doubly sure that you have everything you need (including extension cords, easels, even a projection screen); you can't afford to assume there will be anything in the forbidden room except an expectant audience. One professional made the mistake of assuming there would be a projection screen in a board room to which he was denied access until the moment of the presentation, and ended up showing his computer slide show on the back of a mounted drawing held by a colleague. Needless to say, the impression left with the board was not one of competence and foresight.

Understanding the Mechanics

Once you have a basic understanding of the room itself, preferably well in advance of your presentation, you need to think through (or rethink) the basic mechanics of your presentation. "Basic mechanics" here refers to everything connected with your presentation from setup to teardown—and especially that part in between. Basic mechanics are often overlooked because they deal with the commonplace—everyone knows how to plug in a projector, to set up an easel, right? Well, maybe. But what if your office just purchased a new set of easels you've never used before, or you're stuck with an old set that's missing a few pieces? Are there outlets in the room where you need them? Are there any outlets at all? What is your projector going to sit on? Few design teams think to bring a rolling projection cart with them to the presentation room (but hats off to the few who do).

You should consider the layout of the room itself. Is it arranged in a way that is conducive to your style of presentation: informal, engaging, and interactive? Often, clients set up presentation rooms with a row of tables for your team and a row of tables for their panel, separated by a gulf of empty space. Can you modify the room layout without offending the client? If you can't, consider parking your nonpresenters at the table and using the space in between as your stage. Above all, don't stand behind your table to talk; do something to break down the physical separation between you and the audience. If you can get them out from behind their barricade, then do it. A good tactic is to have a model or drawing that is too small for them to see if they stay seated—make them get out of their chairs to come look at it. As with many things in business, when it comes to rearranging a presentation room, it is much easier to get forgiveness than permission.

Of course, should you choose to redecorate the presentation room, you owe it to your client (and your competitors, if a marketing presentation) to put things back the way you found them when your presentation is over. Think how good it will feel rebuilding the barricades separated by a carpeted gulch knowing that the next team into the room won't think to rearrange them!

Managing the Lighting

The ultimate component of finding your light is…finding your light. When your advance team is surveying the room in which you are to present, take note of the lighting. Is the lighting fluorescent, incandescent, or indirect, or some combination of the three? How is it controlled? If possible, set up your projector (if you are using one), and check the various lighting possibilities for the best balance of light between you and on your visuals. If you are using presentation boards, find an area where they will be lit as evenly as possible. In low-ceiling spaces, setting boards under downlights may create harsh hot spots and dark, scalloped shadows. If there is track lighting in the room, try to realign it to show you and your visual aids to the best effect. Consider unscrewing a bulb (if it can be done safely) that casts an unwanted glare on your screen (just remember to screw it back in when you are done).

Most important of all, study the light levels in the room to help you decide where to stand. You may not be able to do anything at all about a room's available light sources, but you can always manage to stand somewhere else. Look on the floor for pools of light, and mentally map the locations where you can and can't be seen. Alert your fellow presenters to these locations as well. But recognize that a light shining on the top of your head, while making you visible, is not necessarily the most flattering light. Try to stand in the half of a downlight's circle of illumination that is farthest from the audience so that more light is on your front side.

If your presentation demands that you dim the lights at some point, designate a light monitor to handle the switches. It's astonishing how many architects expect the lights to dim themselves at the appropriate moment—so far, no telepathic dimming hardware is in the electrical designer's arsenal. In general, it is preferable to leave the lights at one setting throughout the presentation. But if dimming the lights is a necessity, make sure the light monitor knows his or her cues—the particular points in your presentation for dimming (and brightening) the lights—so that you don't have to plead, "If we could have the lights, please." And, obviously, don't dim the lights until it's absolutely necessary. There is no point speaking in a darkened room any longer than you absolutely have to.

The ideal lighting setup, to the degree that there is such a thing, would be different for presentations involving mounted drawings and projected images.

Where to Find the Worst Lighting for Presenting

Ironically, the worst lighting for presentations will often be found in meeting rooms in convention and conference centers—whose primary use is to host presentations. Even rooms that have three sets of lights (fluorescent, downlights, and cove lighting) and six or more preset light levels often fail to provide adequate light for speakers. This is because, no matter how many lighting systems and controls a room has, if the speaker's vertical surfaces (face and body) are not illuminated, he or she is not well lit. Ask a theatrical lighting designer how effective his or her stage lighting would be if all the lighting had to come from directly above the actors.

How can this be? How can the design profession continue to crank out inferior lighting for rooms in which the presentation of lectures, seminars, and papers is the primary function? Charitably, it can be assumed the reason is that the designers of the space have never had to give a presentation. More likely, it's because the architect and lighting designers are frustrated by the multipurpose nature of these spaces, and hence, are unable (or unwilling) to speculate where speakers might be standing in order to adequately light them.

But just in case you ever have the opportunity to design a convention center meeting room, here are a couple of unsolicited lighting design tips:

▶ Nine times out of ten, the presenter will be at the wall opposite the main set of entry doors. When rooms are combined, the presenter will usually be at the end of the space.

▶ The critical idea is to get light on the speaker's face and body (the vertical surface), not the top of his or her head. To do this requires light coming from an angle.

▶ Generally speaking, a 30-degree angle from the horizontal is best for illuminating the vertical surfaces of a speaker.

▶ Lighting for speakers should leave some dark areas along the same wall where a large projection screen can be located.

For projection, the ideal scenario would be a moderate level of ambient light, to allow the audience to see each other and their notes, with a fairly strong wash of light on you and your team members (see the sidebar discussion, "Where to Find the Worst Lighting for Presentations"). For static displays, a fairly high level of ambient lighting would be preferable, without noticeable gaps in coverage. In a brightly lit room, you need worry less about where to stand, giving you more freedom of movement. In both cases, daylight must be managed to prevent either glare or silhouetting from distracting your audience.

Summing It Up

Finding your light means, first of all, understanding the setting where your presentation is to be given. There is no excuse for walking into a room and being surprised that the conditions you find there are unsuitable for the presentation you are planning to give. Finding your light includes paying attention to:

- ▶ Understanding the physical location of the presentation—room layout, furnishings, acoustical conditions, and other factors affecting your presentation.

- ▶ Dealing with rooms that are too large (by tightening up the furnishings) or too small (by constraining the size and scope of your presentation).

- ▶ Dealing with complications resulting from unwanted daylight—avoiding being in silhouette and avoiding glare on projected images.

- ▶ Sending a person or team (preferably, including yourself) to scout the location ahead of time.

- ▶ Managing the mechanics of your presentation so that you have thought through all the details (who sets up what, where things plug in) prior to your entering the room to give the presentation.

➤ Understanding and managing the lighting in a presentation room—knowing where the controls are and how they work, and testing to determine the best lighting for the presentation you plan to give.

➤ When given the opportunity, designing presentation rooms with better lighting.

Delivering Your Presentation

Part II

Face Out

5

Another correction the inexperienced actor frequently hears called out in rehearsal from the darkened seats of an auditorium is the admonition to "Face out!" Facing out has several dimensions that are discussed in this chapter, but in its most basic sense it means keeping your front side oriented toward the audience at all times. "All times" here should be understood in a nonabsolute way: it doesn't mean that you should never ever turn your back to the audience, but that you should never turn your back to them for more than a moment. "Out" means out toward the audience.

Of all presenters, architects and designers are among the worst at facing out. Why? Because we are often presenting drawings or other images of our work, and it is much easier (and, let's be honest, less frightening) to talk to our drawings than to talk to the audience. So while facing out may seem an obvious rule for presenters, it is one that architects struggle to observe, often failing badly.

Interestingly, the injunction to face out does not mean that you should square up to the audience and

TIP
(Almost) never turn your back on the audience.

address them as if you were a candidate for student council. Your presentation—the dance—will be more interesting and engaging if you face out at a slight angle, using movement (as described in Chapter 1) to orient your body toward different sections of the audience at different times. Facing squarely out can lock you into a static posture that will quickly become boring to the audience and a trap from which you may find it difficult to escape.

Cheating Out

A corollary direction to "facing out" is "cheating out," which is the position stage actors take when they are supposed to be interacting with one another. Unless they're at a ball game, most people square up for conversation and look directly at each other. In stage presentations, this would result in the actors' being too much in profile for the bulk of the audience, and actually showing their backs to people seated to the left and right of center. So actors are told to cheat out, that is, to open up the angle between their bodies so that they appear to be in conversation, but are actually forming a broad V that lets the audience in on the interaction (see Figure 5.1). In a sense, the audience becomes the third member of the conversation. Cheating out has obvious implications for presenters, particularly when you have more than one person presenting at the same time. Use the idea of cheating out to include your audience in the discussion among your team members.

The Five E's

Beyond the obvious question of which way your body is pointing, there are several different dimen-

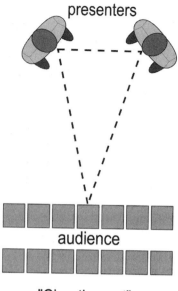

presenters

audience

"Cheating out"

Figure 5.1

sions of facing out to be concerned with. These dimensions have to do with showing regard for your audience as people, and with creating a lively and memorable piece of performance art for them.

The five E's are:

- ► Energy
- ► Empathy
- ► Enthusiasm
- ► Engagement
- ► Entertainment

By learning to cultivate these five qualities, you will eliminate boredom from your presentations and go a long way toward making them livelier and more compelling.

Energy

A characteristic that every performer desires to bring to the stage is energy. One of the worst things you can say to a performer is that his or her performance lacked energy. But what is "energy" in the context of performance art? And how does that relate to architects making oral presentations?

One school of thought holds that energy is some magical spiritual quality that, like a ballplayer's being "in the zone," you either have it or you don't, and there's no telling when you might get it or when it might go away. This view, which is fairly prevalent in the performing arts, is both fatalistic and flawed, because if energy is a quality that is external to the performer, then the actor has no responsibility for its presence or absence. Rather, energy (or lack of it) becomes a way to rationalize performances that go well (or badly) for reasons the actor doesn't fully understand.

Another way to look at energy, however, is by using a musical metaphor. When music is slow, syrupy, and pitched in the lower ranges of our hearing, we tend to think of it as boring. Classical music labeled "adagio" is often thought of as uninteresting, at least by nonconnoisseurs. On the other hand, music that is up-tempo and filled with bright, brassy sound is said to be high energy (contemporary dance music, for example). This leads to a fairly simple formula for the public speaker: energy, as with music, is simply a function of pitch and pace; that is:

$$Energy = Pitch + Pace$$

Pitch, technically, is the frequency (in cycles per second) that your vocal cords are vibrating to create sound. Men usually operate their voices at a much lower pitch than women, which puts men at a distinct disadvantage in the energy department. Imagine for a moment that you heard the same 30-second commercial read by a deep-voiced male and a typically voiced female. Which reading would you likely think had more energy, assuming they read the same number of words in the allotted time? Most people would answer the female's reading would have more energy. Consequently, male presenters need to be more thoughtful about the energy level they are projecting in their presentations. Female presenters, on the other hand, need to be cautious about talking too fast, or they may come across as too intense for the audience. Generally, though, most design presentations are far more likely to be judged as lacking energy as to having an excessive amount of it.

Pace is the other half of the energy equation. Pace is simply the rate at which the words come out of your mouth—obviously, more words per unit of time equals faster pace. Now if energy is acknowledged as a good quality to cultivate in your presentations, then faster talking is better, right? Well, to a point. Again, speaking generally, most design professionals talk far too slowly, but that is not to say it's impossible to talk too fast. It's unlikely, but not impossible.

Another aspect of pace to mention is that while, in general, faster is better, it's not good to run your presentation spiel at the same rate for its entire length. Variety of pace is important to avoid monotony. Audiences can become bored with even rapid-fire delivery of a message if the rate of delivery never changes. So if you are consciously speeding up your presentation delivery (to gain in the energy department), think of several places to slow down to

 TIP

To give your presentation energy, you have to increase either the pitch of your voice or the pace at which you talk.

TIP

Vary your pace to keep your presentation from becoming one-dimensional.

emphasize important points. Or stop altogether for a moment to let a point sink in. Your audience will appreciate it.

The mystical view of energy described earlier is accurate in one respect: that is, except for the most veteran and professional performers, one rarely knows in advance what level of energy will be seen by the audience. That is because few presenters are able to gauge their rate of delivery with stopwatch accuracy, and because that rate will vary between rehearsal and "the real thing." What can be predicted is that the rate at which you talk in a live presentation will, like your heart rate, generally be faster than in rehearsal—but you will also say more. So don't plan on saving any time in a presentation by talking faster than you normally do. Timing is discussed further in Chapter 10, "Know When to Get Off."

Empathy

> *"If a knucklehead like me can be president, and do all right, think what a smart guy like you could do."*
> —HARRY TRUMAN (to Adlai Stevenson)

Possibly the most important of the five E's, empathy is difficult for many presenters to achieve, and especially so for design professionals. Achieving empathy requires establishing an emotional connection with your audience, so that they relate to you as a person, not just as a dispenser of information.

In technical presentations, there is a natural tendency to launch right in to the critical points and cover the material that needs to be covered. While this is understandable, failure by a presenter to establish an empathetic connection with his or her audience will make it difficult, if not impossible, to achieve his or her objective. Empathy is the quality that brings the audience over to your side, that gets them pulling for you, that makes them want you to be successful. Needless to say, these are desirable outcomes, and vastly preferable to any alternative.

So how do you begin to develop empathy with your audience? There are several possible strategies to consider and employ:

TIP

Establish an emotional connection with the audience right away.

- ► *Begin by talking about yourself.* This may sound strange, especially if you are about to launch into a detailed technical presentation, but you should always begin with a personal glimpse into the person behind the suit. Beginning with a brief personal note does several things: it lets the audience into your life, to know you as a person before they know you as a professional; it can provide a brief moment of humor to lighten the mood; it can even engender sympathy.

- ► *Begin with a humorous personal story* (as opposed to a joke; see "Entertainment" below). Laughter is a great tension reliever, and if the story describes something slightly embarrassing that happened to you, the audience will see that you're not a stuffed shirt.

- ► *Use self-deprecating humor throughout your presentation.* Obvious as it may seem, many presenters unwisely direct pointed, sarcastic, or biting remarks at targets other than themselves. This is dangerous and ill-advised. Misdirected satire marks you as critical, smug, and condescending. Better to copy the example of the Wichita attorney who started every summation with the statement, "Now, I may just be a dumb ole country lawyer, but...." It bears mentioning that *you* are the only good target for self-deprecating remarks.

Making fun of other members of your team will not gain any more empathy than if you were to criticize members of the audience.

▶ *Find points of connection with your audience.* If you are a middle-aged male presenting to a room full of middle-aged males, this may not be difficult. But in today's business environment, likely as not there will be significant age, gender, or cultural differences between you and your audience. You need to think—ahead of time—of topics that can bridge the gap. Depending on circumstances, this may include talking about hobbies, cultural events (discussing a popular television show is a technique that can work with almost any audience that's not Amish), the weather, or any topic common to you and your hearers. Why do so many stand-up comedians do routines about air travel? Because most adults have been on an airplane at least once in their lives.

▶ *Share some observations about the project, the site, or the client, to show you have common interests and experiences.* For example, one presenter began a talk by saying, "It was interesting to learn that this university is a land-grant institution, because the college I went to was also a land-grant school." As superficial as these observations seem, they create at least one connection between you and your audience from which to build your case and achieve your objective.

Enthusiasm

Everyone knows of at least one project that was won by a less-qualified firm on the enthusiasm of their presentation. What is enthusiasm, and how can you bottle it so that it's ready to use in the meeting room?

A Tale of Two Architects

At a recent AIA National Convention, delegates were treated to a pair of back-to-back architectural presentations that, taken together, were a powerful lesson in how to build empathy—and how not to. The Gold Medalist addressed a general assembly of the convention, followed in short order by the invited keynote speaker. The Gold Medalist was charming, humble, humorous, and winning, while the keynote speaker was anything but. Both speakers gave presentations that were similar in content (a brief illustrated retrospective of their work), but the Gold Medalist delivered his with wit and polish, at one point joking, "We Mexicans are irresponsible in our use of color," to explain his brightly colored buildings.

The keynote speaker began her talk by disparaging the greenery used to decorate the platform at the convention: "I hate nature," she said, and few in the audience were entirely sure she was joking. Her presentation of her work, which is characteristically challenging, was punctuated with insults directed toward the offstage technicians who were attempting to keep up with her stream-of-consciousness discussion. The keynote speaker won few fans at the convention with her terse presentation style.

Enthusiasm is, quite literally, the spirit within you. Every person has a spirit, an unembodied personal power that directs our lives. Letting that spirit show through is the essence of enthusiasm. Unfortunately, enthusiasm is often stifled in the presentation context by a variety of competing forces: nerves, tension, fear, anxiety, doubt, temporary paralysis, and detailed technical content all conspire to restrain your enthusiasm.

So how can you store up the natural enthusiasm you feel for your work to bring out at the crucial moment in a presentation? Sadly, enthusiasm can't be canned, and it can't be faked. But there are several things you can do to allow the spirit you want to project to your audience out of its container (you):

REMINDER

One of the biggest obstacles to enthusiasm is tension felt by the presenter.

- Do your physical warm-ups (see Chapter 1) so that your enthusiasm is not restrained by physical tension and stress.

- Be mentally prepared to talk (see Chapter 3), so that your enthusiasm is not subjugated to needless worry about what you're going to say.

- Take command of the space for your presentation so that you are seen as a positive leader, not just a talking head.

- Keep your energy level up (see above) by talking a little bit faster than usual, and by being aware of your pitch.

- Stay away from sedatives—especially alcohol—that dull your reactions and make your thought and speech cloudy.

If you are genuinely unhappy about giving a talk, that will be as evident to your audience as it is to you. Consider whether you really have to give the speech, whether someone else might be able to cover for you and do a better job, or whether you might be setting yourself up to fail by giving a presentation for which you are not able to adequately prepare. On the other hand, by using the above techniques, you can remove most of the major obstacles to letting your natural enthusiasm for your work come through.

Not the Cheerleader Type?

One objection to cultivating enthusiasm in presentations comes from mild-mannered people who feel constitutionally incapable of enthusiasm. "I know I should be more enthusiastic when I present," they say, "but it's just not me. I'm not the cheerleader type." Are you being asked to wear a short skirt and carry pom-poms into the presentation? No. Enthusiasm is about being yourself, not about jumping up and down and yelling at the top of your lungs. But what if, as many protest, just being yourself is a little too subdued for the desired result?

In various twelve-step recovery programs, there is a saying, "Fake it 'til you make it." This expression, which may strike you as being extremely cynical, is a useful tip for generating enthusiasm. If you know that your past is littered with presentations where you have been too bland or seemed to lack excitement, psych yourself up using the bullet points above as a guide. "I will be physically prepared to present. I will have a mastery of my subject that allows me to talk without notes. I will take charge of the space. I will talk a little faster than usual." But don't just say those words to yourself: do them. If you have to make a conscious effort to ratchet up the energy level a notch a few times, so be it. With enough practice speaking (remember the Practice Paradox?), you will eventually become an enthusiastic presenter; that is, not a presenter who looks like someone who has been on an intravenous espresso drip all day, but one who pleasantly and naturally conveys the excitement he or she feels about the project, or his or her firm, or the topic of the speech.

Engagement

Another critical "E" is learning to engage your audience. You can have absolute mastery of a subject, but if you fail to engage the audience in your talk, you will be perceived as dry, boring, or, even worse, a know-it-all. Engagement and empathy are two magic ingredients that are sadly lacking from the vast majority of presentations by design professionals. This is because architects and designers often fail to recognize the two-way nature of oral communication. Giving a speech, as has been stated before, is not just an information dump. It is a dance between the speaker and the audience, where both entities take a crucial part.

Many postinterview discussions center around each presenter's opinion of how engaged the listeners seemed to be. Was there frequent eye contact, were heads nodding in agreement, were there empathetic smiles? It's easy to tell when the audience is not engaged: when they sit stone-faced and immobile, looking as if they hope you'll finish talking so they can go to lunch. But what does it really mean to get an audience engaged in a presentation?

RULE OF THUMB

Engagement is the art of drawing your listeners into your story and making it a part of their experience.

Engagement is the art of drawing your listeners into your story, making it not just a part of their aural environment, but a part of their life. There are two principal strategies for achieving a high level of engagement: interaction and interrogation. Each will be discussed briefly below.

Interaction

The importance of interaction has already been mentioned, in the section titled "Presentation Formats" in Chapter 2. One key to achieving engagement is choosing a presentation format that allows for the maximum degree of interaction with your audience. Interaction is critical to engagement.

Of course, many times the presentation format is dictated by your client, which makes a high level of interaction difficult. In those circumstances, you must make an extra effort to make members of the audience a part of the discussion. To fail to do so is to forgo one of the most effective tools you have as a presenter.

At the simplest level, interaction is simply bringing audience members into the discussion. You do this most often by asking questions (see "Interrogation" below). But in order to ask questions, you need to give yourself and your audience permission to interact in the first place. In theater, this is called "breaking down the fourth wall," the barrier that exists between actor and audience. To break down the fourth wall, you should do one or more of the following:

- ► If you're standing, sit down.

- ► If you're on a platform, get off of it.

- ► Pull up a chair next to your audience.

- ► If your audience is seated, find an excuse to make them stand up.

- ► Violate the "stage" boundary by walking into or behind the audience.

Will some of these strategies make you harder to see? Yes. Will they make some audience members have to crane around in their seats to find you? Yes. Isn't that a violation of the principles discussed in Chapter 4, "Find Your Light"? Yes. But interaction is so critical to achieving engagement that it merits breaking some of the basic rules of presenting to achieve it.

You may at some time in your life have seen a production of the 1970's era musical *Godspell*, which was very popular with amateur theater groups after its initial Broadway run. In almost every production of *Godspell*, the first thing that happens after the lights go down is that the actors enter from the back of the auditorium and walk (or run) down the aisles singing, "Prepare Ye the Way of the Lord," the first number in the show. This staging decision is startling (at least the first time), and lets the audience know right away that *Godspell* isn't your basic Rodgers and Hammerstein production. In fact, *Godspell* is one of the most interactive musicals ever produced, during which the audience often becomes a part of the action. While this technique waxes and wanes in popularity in the theater, it is a surefire winner in public presentations.

Team Interaction

Another type of interaction is between members of your design team, assuming you are not doing a solo presentation. The interaction between team members can tell your audience a lot about the chemistry of the group, particularly in hiring interviews. Generally, multiple presenters relate to each other stiffly, if at all, whereas good team interaction consists of banter, thoughtful interruption, and piggybacking.

Banter is just the byplay between a group of professionals who like each other and who like working together. Banter is difficult to fake, because it requires genuine affection not to come across as one-upmanship or heckling. A simple comment like, "This is John's first encounter with a laptop computer," can be seen as warm and friendly or bitterly sarcastic depending on the real relationship between the participants. So be careful to banter with people you know and like, and save your biting sarcasm for the postgame session in the bar.

Thoughtful interruption is a most helpful kind of team interaction. Done well, it helps everyone stay focused on the objective of the presentation. Done poorly, it can make the interrupter seem controlling and rude. The essence of thoughtful interruption is to redirect a point of the discussion in real time.

Examples of thoughtful interruption include cutting short a consultant whose discourse on lighting controls has gone on too long; reminding a colleague that the audience is there to hear about their project, not your vacation in France; or correcting a factual error made by a senior partner who is not up to date on the latest details of the project. As you can see, all these examples involve the risk of coming across as a jerk, so you must interrupt with the utmost of care and diplomacy, but thoughtful interruptions can actually help a presentation stay on course. Of course, if you are the one being thoughtfully interrupted, you need to manage your reactions: avoid defensive or dismissive responses ("Of course, I knew that") and welcome the interruption as valuable input from a valuable member of your professional team.

Piggybacking is perhaps the simplest form of team interaction. It is simply building on one another's thoughts in a dynamic way. If something another presenter says gives you a good idea, add it to the discussion. If you are the presenter, invite your colleagues to pile on with their additional comments. The only downside to piggybacking is the risk of becoming so absorbed in a dynamic discussion that you lose track of time in your presentation and end up missing key points that come later. In order to prevent this, build extra time into parts of your presentation where piggybacking is most likely to occur.

Interrogation

The other technique for engaging your audience is to position yourself as an interrogator. This does not mean, obviously, shining hot lights in their faces and pressuring them to confess to criminal acts. It does mean asking a series of questions from the innocuous ("How are you doing today?") to the fairly serious ("What's most important to you about the project we're discussing?"). When you ask questions, you are inviting the audience to respond. Getting the audience to respond is the only way to know for certain that they are engaged in the discussion.

The objection is often raised at this point, "What if I ask a question and no one answers?" The short answer is that if that should happen, your audience is obviously not engaged in your discussion. But the better answer is to wait. Both presenters and audience members are uncomfortable with silence, and a few seconds will seem like an eternity, but eventually one of your listeners will break down and offer up an opinion. It helps if you start with questions that are fairly nonthreatening ("Give me a word that describes your campus") and don't require deep introspection. Save those for when the interrogation is farther along.

It may seem odd to suggest asking questions in a presentation where your primary goal is to convey a lot of information about yourself, your project, or your firm. But it is only through questions that you can determine whether the information that is most critical is getting through. And it is only through questions that you can determine which information is most important to your audience, as opposed to information that you think is important to your audience. The difference is highly significant.

The main thing to remember is that for a presentation to be engaging, it needs to be more of a conversation than a monologue. And a conversation requires a minimum of two parties. If you have good interaction among members of your design team, that's a plus, but if that's all you have, you still have not achieved engagement with the audience. Make achieving engagement a goal for your next presentation, and for each presentation you give afterward.

Entertainment

We come now to the fifth of the five E's, entertainment. Of all the various aspects of facing out, of gaining audience empathy and support, of combating boredom and dullness, entertainment is the most challenging for architects and designers. Architects are not, by and large, entertainers by nature. Some designers would even question the need for entertainment in a technical presentation. The late Peter Glen, in a column in *VM+SD* magazine, made a compelling case for entertainment when he said:

> I know that if people are having fun at my presentations, they are absorbing twice as much as if the same material were being delivered witlessly. If they are laughing, they are learning. . . . FUN makes the transmission of ideas palatable.

There are several reasons why Glen's comment is so valid. Most apparently, a person having fun is more likely to be alert and tuned in than one who is bored. Also, entertainment can help break the tension in a room and help people relax and feel more at ease. Obviously, relaxation (on either the audience's or the speaker's part) is conducive to achieving your objective, especially compared to feelings of tension and anxiety. Using entertainment properly can make your presentation more memorable, particularly in a competitive setting. Finally, and perhaps most significantly, entertainment requires a risk on your part, showing an aspect of your personality that may not otherwise be apparent in a presentation. This risk-taking is a critical part of the dance, as your audience wants you to reveal yourself, your true nature, to them.

TIP

Using entertainment properly can make your presentation more memorable, particularly in a competitive setting.

That's Entertainment—Not

It's probably worth pointing out a few types of entertainment that are not appropriate for any presentation, professional or otherwise. In the not-too-distant-past, when the practice of architecture was mainly an old boys' club (and where most of the boys were the same age and ethnicity), telling off-color jokes was a standard bonding tool, a way of achieving empathy by defining a "them" that was fundamentally different from "us" (the boys in the room). Needless to say, those days are long gone. Telling off-color jokes is a surefire way to lose the confidence of any client or public agency, even in rural areas where such humor was last seen alive.

Likewise, the use of inappropriate imagery, including pornographic images, is similarly strongly discouraged. Images of people who are bizarrely dressed or culturally stereotyped in any way should be excluded from your presentation, because it's likely that someone you're talking to will either identify with the object of ridicule or know someone who does. This puts you in the unpleasant position of poking fun at your listeners, a position to avoid at all costs. One speaker got in trouble for doing an impersonation of Don Knotts as Deputy Barney Fife with an audience of southerners, at least one of whom thought he was poking fun at rural southerners. Such are the multiple sensitivities of the modern audience.

That's Entertainment

With so many taboo subjects, it's reasonable to ask what options remain for providing entertainment in a talk. Fortunately, several possibilities exist. A few of them are listed below:

▶ *Jokes at your own expense.* Self-deprecating humor, you'll recall from the discussion of empathy above, is just about the safest kind.

▶ *Amusing stories of your own experiences,* or experiences that might have happened to you (that is, anecdotes that actually happened to someone else but are amusing enough to appropriate for your own use).

▶ *Travel photos that might have some bearing on the topic at hand.* While not directly relevant to the project or your firm, your vacation photos from Sri Lanka can add a lot of color and vitality to an otherwise drab presentation, particularly if you can make some connection to the real topic. Just be careful to use your travel images as ornament, not to insert an entirely separate talk on Sri Lanka within your real presentation.

▶ *Joke-book jokes.* Bookstores are full of collections of appropriate humor, from which it is not difficult to select one or two that have some connection, however loose, to the subject at hand. ("Interviewing for this post office project reminds me of the story of the letter carrier who....") Just be careful to remember the guidelines above about inappropriate content. If the joke involves a naked housewife or a rabbi, forget about it.

▶ *Amusing topical news.* This is a great entertainment device, because it is current (joke-book jokes can sound dated) and because there is a chance some or all of your audience already know the story. You can take material from talk show hosts, as long as it meets the appropriateness rule (and as long as you don't start performing it at open-mike nights at the local comedy club).

➤ *Humor you create on your own.* (See the sidebar, "How to Be Funny.") Admittedly a challenging undertaking, consider whether there is something about your audience, your location, your topic, or yourself that lends itself to an entertaining send-up (done with the utmost sensitivity, of course). One format that is widely copied is David Letterman's Top Ten List from his late-night talk show. You can do "Top Ten Amazing Facts about [Meeting Site]," "Top Ten Little-Known Facts about Our Firm," and so on. The key is to keep it light, keep it brief, and get on with the program. Don't make humor the focal point of your presentation; make it the counterpoint to your main theme, which might in fact be quite serious.

➤ *More diverse forms of entertainment.* Here are several out-of-the-box techniques some firms have used (mostly in marketing work) to set themselves apart from the pack:

♦ Using loud rock music to underscore team introductions.

♦ Singing the school's fight song.

♦ Having pizza delivered midway through the presentation (be sure that a strategy like this isn't illegal from the client's point of view).

♦ Beginning a presentation with the patter song "Ya Got Trouble" from Meredith Wilson's *The Music Man.*

♦ Getting the participants to play with Legos or building blocks.

How to Be Funny

"Dying is easy; comedy is hard," goes the old saying. Anyone who has ever had a joke fall flat on its face can affirm the sentiment. But being funny, like so many other aspects of presenting, is not a black art that requires some genetic predisposition to funniness. It is a matter of taking ordinary conversation and giving it a twist. One basic suggestion: the punch line comes at the end. Make sure that what's funny about your amusing anecdote is the very last thing you say. Following are four basic methods of making a story into a humorous one:

- ➤ *Observation.* Some stories are funny in and of themselves. Like the sign on the office building door that says, "No Soliciting." The key is to take note of things that are offbeat, then develop a compact approach to describing them. Just remember that observations about the audience's character will not help you build empathy with them.

- ➤ *Exaggeration.* Sometimes reality needs a helping hand. Use analogy and metaphor to give a larger impact to people and situations that we all experience and understand everyday. Example: "Definition of a nanosecond: the time period from when the traffic light turns green and the driver behind you honks the horn."

- ➤ *Sudden Twist.* A basic element of the joke or humorous story is that something changes at the end that takes the listener in an entirely different direction. The classic example is the Henny Youngman chestnut, "Take my wife...please." That one extra word, unexpected and out of left field, changes the entire meaning of what came before. Most sudden-twist jokes have more than four words, of course, but compactness is always a virtue in comedy.

- ➤ *Equivocation.* This logic term is fundamental to a number of comedic approaches. It means that somewhere along the way, the meaning of one of the terms in an argument is changed. For example, in the old standup routine, "Call me a taxi." "Okay, you're a taxi," the verb "call" is equivocated from meaning "summon" in the first line to "name" in the punch line. Many classic humorous bits are based on equivocation, including the legendary "Who's on First?" performed innumerable times by Bud Abbott and Lou Costello.

Writing comedy, like any discipline, takes practice. But it is not an unattainable gift or an art that is beyond mere mortals. You may not want to go into stand-up comedy as a second career, but what speech would not benefit from a few well-placed zingers to keep the audience awake? Have you ever heard a really good speech that *didn't* include a few good jokes?

> *Use a computer-generated video of the project or the environment or your firm's work to fire up the audience.* A more thorough discussion of video follows in Chapter 9, "Remember Your Props." Make sure the video has a soundtrack—nothing minimizes the excitement factor like a silent movie.

> *Have a celebrity endorser talk about your team or your project.* Sometimes, you know someone who, though not qualified to be a part of your team, would give your team a boost just by talking about it. If you can capture that promotional minute on videotape, it can make an entertaining launch (or finish) to a presentation. Just be sure that your endorser doesn't ramble. Edit his or her remarks if necessary—two minutes can seem like an eternity when everyone is watching a video image of someone talking.

Summing It Up

Facing out involves recognizing that the interaction taking place in your presentation is first and foremost between the presenter and the audience. It means being aware of, and taking into account, the audience's composition, mood, feelings, and comfort. And it involves a number of intangibles, which are summarized in this book as the five E's:

> *Energy.* The combination of pitch (frequency) and pace (words per minute) that make you seem to be either a motivated speaker or a bore.

> *Empathy.* Establishing an emotional connection with your audience through the identification of common traits or experiences or the use of self-deprecating humor. Empathy may be the

most critical intangible in achieving your talk's objective.

- ► *Engagement.* Making the audience a part of your talk. Use the tools of interaction and interrogation to foster active participation by the listeners, to draw them into your discussion, and to make your presentation into a conversation, rather than a monologue.

- ► *Enthusiasm.* The spirit you bring to a presentation is the most difficult thing to fake, but sometimes forcing yourself to behave with enthusiasm will help generate this internal energy. Being physically prepared to present ("showing up," Chapter 1) will help release the enthusiasm you naturally have for your work.

- ► *Entertainment.* For many architects, the most challenging of the five E's is making their presentations entertaining, because entertainment is seldom a part of their training or experience. Entertainment does not have to mean telling jokes, however; you can add entertainment to a presentation with anecdotes, travel pictures, video, or even song and dance. Entertaining presentations can be clinically proven to be more effective than nonentertaining presentations.

Keep Going

6

One of the most jarring things you can experience in a theater, more jarring than nudity or gunfire or Michael Jackson, is when the show stops. Not because of sustained applause (this kind of show-stopping is a good thing), but because something has gone so horribly wrong that the performance cannot continue. A show can stop for a variety of reasons: disaster, fire alarm, illness or injury to one of the players, power failure, and so on, but when it does, it's equally disturbing for both performers and audience. When the show stops, even briefly, the illusion is broken and people are faced with the sudden, jarring realization that they are seated in a theater but no longer watching a performance, where a moment before they were so enthralled with the reality the performers were creating that they were blissfully unaware of the artifice.

Obviously, stopping the show under any circumstance is not desirable. The consequences of a break in the action, however brief, are deadly to the quality of almost any performance. That's why one of the ten commandments of show business is to *keep going*.

RULE OF THUMB

The consequences of a break in the action, however brief, are deadly to the quality of almost any performance.

Whether someone flubs a line, misses a cue, or slams a door; or a siren goes by outside or a light burns out—any minor mishap that does not endanger the audience or the performers is simply overlooked. To do otherwise is to risk breaking character, dispelling the illusion, losing the magical moment created by the performance thus far.

Sadly, many presenters don't understand this fundamental rule of show business. They become flustered at the slightest difficulty, shut down a presentation for the weakest of reasons, and generally have no sense of how interruptions can literally let the air out of an otherwise effective presentation. And here's a news flash: stuff happens. Every presenter, every time he or she presents, is faced with unexpected obstacles, large and small, intentional or not, that can derail a train of thought faster than a cow on the tracks. This chapter deals with some of those obstacles and issues facing presenters and gives sensible strategies for overcoming them. The most important strategy of all, however, is the commandment itself: Unless someone is in real danger, keep going.

TIP

The most important strategy is: Unless someone is in real danger, keep going.

Overcoming Obstacles

There are numerous obstacles that can conspire to derail a presentation. These include the mundane (a projector bulb burns out) to the pernicious (people in your audience jumping up to answer their cell phones). In one sense, every obstacle is serious in that it presents the opportunity for your presentation to go off course. In another, no obstacle is so serious that you should let it (unless, of course, there is a real threat to life and limb).

There are, in essence, two types of obstacles: those you can plan for, and those you can't. Obviously, you should plan for as many of the predictable obstacles as possible.

Expectable Obstacles

Back in the days when most architects used slide projectors to talk about their work, no self-respecting architect would go to a presentation without a spare projector lamp in his or her pocket. Some even had exotic two-lamp projectors where a spare could be brought on-line in a moment. And every self-respecting architect in those days understood Murphy's Law with respect to slide projectors: Anything that can go wrong, will go wrong, and always at the worst possible moment.

TIP

You should plan for as many predictable obstacles as possible.

But slide projectors, while still common today, are being displaced by liquid crystal display (LCD) projectors connected to laptop computers. And this combination presents a dilemma: There are even more things to go wrong, and the average design professional is even less qualified to fix them. LCD projectors often use special lamps that cost hundreds of dollars; few architects travel with a spare in their pocket, and most wouldn't know how to change the lamp if they did. Fortunately, these lamps have extremely long life cycles, but they do fail, and as Murphy's Law predicts, they will fail at the worst possible time.

The point of this discussion is not that you should bring two LCD projectors to every presentation (although if you could, it might not be a bad idea). The point is that since equipment failure is possible, and since it is capable of being anticipated, there is no excuse for not having a backup plan. In the case of a computer/LCD projector show, this could be as simple as having overhead transparencies in an envelope for when the technology gremlins have their way with you. All you have to do is ensure that there is an overhead projector in the room, something most meeting venues have readily available. There is no reason why your presentation should be derailed by obstacles you could reasonably have been expected to anticipate.

Other examples of expectable obstacles include the overnight shipment of handouts that fails to arrive, the flight that fails to arrive at your destination on time (maybe you should have gone the night before!), the room with unfathomable lighting controls (recall the discussion on "Find Your Light" in Chapter 4), the wall that's not long enough to display all your exhibits, the easel with a missing part, the senior principal who always forgets how long he or she is supposed to talk, the presentation schedule with no setup time included, and so on. Every one of these problems has a solution that can be thought through well in advance.

In a certain sense, your ability to deal with expectable difficulties is a mark of your fitness to accomplish the task you are presenting about—presumably the qualifications of your firm or the characteristics of a project you have in design. Everyone knows that construction is a messy, unpredictable process—much messier and more unpredictable than presenting, in fact—and how you handle the small annoyances that plague any presentation is an indicator of how your firm will handle the innumerable hurdles that occur in the construction of a project. So the ability to move smoothly from a computer show to an overhead projector (or even to a flip chart or a

Do I Need an Understudy?

In show business, one of the worst obstacles is when a featured performer (or, really, any performer) is unable to take the stage due to injury, illness, or fits of temperament. For this reason, roles in live productions are *understudied* so that an acceptable replacement player is available on short notice—sometimes only the interval between two acts.

While understudies for presentations may seem an extreme idea, design professionals often paint themselves into a corner by viewing themselves as uniquely able to make a presentation. In a functional, cross-trained professional office, it would seem reasonable that if a project designer is unable to attend a presentation, a junior designer would have sufficient mastery of the topic to fill in. If a project manager is indisposed, a project architect ought to be familiar enough with how the project is running or should run to be able to take his or her place. And even if a senior principal is taken out of the game on a critical day, there should be another partner or junior manager who can step up and fill that role.

Understudying requires that these people be present for all, or most, rehearsals leading up to a presentation, and that they understand their responsibility to master the topic as well as the person they may have to replace. Again, the practice of identifying understudies may seem like an extreme measure, but there are enough instances in the lore of the profession of a sudden illness, a missed flight connection, or a crisis on another front taking a key presenter out of the lineup that having an understudy available seems not only wise, but necessary for a critical presentation.

whiteboard) will give your audience a foretaste of how you will react under pressure of construction field problems. Again, reacting to problems is part of the dance.

Unexpected Obstacles

The other type of obstacle that you must overcome is the kind that even the most pessimistic presenter could not have reasonably expected. These include actions by audience members that, while not overtly hostile, can easily cause your train of thought to jump the tracks. For example, it is not unheard of for members of client panels to leave the room in the middle of a presentation, to interrupt with unexpected questions (although by now you should be beginning to think of the unsolicited question as an asset rather than as a liability), or to undermine some major point of your presentation with a sweeping generalization. These hiccups can bring a presentation to a grinding halt as easily as a building power outage.

The question you must ask yourself when such unanticipated disruptions occur—and they will occur, as will others not mentioned above—is, "Does this disruption merit stopping my presentation to deal with it?" For example, if one panelist steps out of the room to take a phone call, it's probably not necessary to stop talking—unless that one person happens to be the key decision maker whose opinion will determine whether or not you reach your objective. In that event, you might say, "Perhaps we should take a short break until [Key Decision Maker] is available again. Would anyone like a warm-up on their coffee?" Recognize that there is a cost associated with stopping a presentation: loss of energy, loss of interest, at times, even loss of participants. You must carefully (and instantly) weigh the cost of stopping with the cost of continuing under less than ideal circumstances.

It's important not to get flustered by these unexpected events, even though they cannot, by their nature, be a part of your prepresentation disaster checklist. This issue will be discussed more thoroughly in Chapter 8, "Be in the Moment." Part of achieving your objective for the presentation depends on how you handle unexpected obstacles.

Overcoming Hostility

One of the things presenters fear greatly is overt hostility on the part of the audience. This is not as far-fetched as it might seem at first glance. Hostility can come from many quarters, particularly in large public forums; but even in small groups there may be a person or two in your audience with a grudge, an attitude, or an ax to grind.

Hostile responses can come in many forms, but two of the most common are the irrelevant speech and the loaded question. Each will be discussed briefly.

Irrelevant Speeches

More common in larger forums, where there is a public audience and sometimes even media in attendance, irrelevant speeches are a form of grandstanding whereby a person attempts to call attention to an issue that is only peripherally related, or perhaps entirely unrelated, to the subject of your presentation. In a volatile political climate, such as one often finds on a college campus, irrelevant speeches are so common as to nearly fall under the heading of "expectable difficulties."

So there you are, innocently pointing out the benefits of the new campus recreation center you're designing, when up pops a hand. Innocently assuming the questioner to have a legitimate interest in your project, you call upon him or her, only to be regaled with a short (or long) speech about how the college should be allocating resources to lowering the outrageously high tuition rates instead of building glorified playpens for coddled students. Your initial reaction might be to react defensively, to engage the interrupter in a debate about the need for campus recreation facilities, but this is likely to only prolong the irrelevancy.

A better response is found in the "AARP" method, an acronym that has nothing to do with retired persons. It stands for a four-step process for dealing with inappropriate feedback: *acknowledge, affirm, record,* and *persevere.*

1. *Acknowledge.* You can't ignore irrelevant speeches. Nothing inflames a touchy situation like a person in charge (in this case you, because you're talking) ignoring a complaint from "the people." You need to acknowledge the speaker and acknowledge the point he or she is trying to make, even if you disagree with it or consider it to be irrelevant to the subject at hand.

2. *Affirm.* This is a critical step. You must learn to affirm irrelevant comments without necessarily agreeing with them. Affirmation is simply letting the speaker know that you got the message and that you understood it. An affirming statement is often just a paraphrase of the irrelevant speech—usually in a lot fewer words. "So I understand you to say that you feel faculty salaries are more important that getting this new facility built? Did I hear you correctly?" In affirming irrelevant speech, make certain that it is the speaker's opinion you are quoting, not your own view of the situation. Affirmation goes a long way toward pacifying belligerent questioners.

3. *Record.* Another key to disarming irrelevant speech is to carefully record it, in a way that can be seen by the speaker. Best is to write it down on a flip chart pad or overhead transparency. This makes the comment a part of the official record of the meeting. If all you have

available is a yellow legal pad, use that, but make a point of painstakingly writing (and reading aloud) your paraphrase of the comment, so that the speaker will know what actually got written down.

4. *Persevere.* Once you have acknowledged the speaker, affirmed that you heard him or her, and recorded a paraphrase of the irrelevant speech, it's time to press on. Further debate at this point will only serve to derail you and call attention to the speaker's issue. If the speaker insists on further debate, be willing to schedule an appointment for him or her to debate you (or the proper authorities) in the future. But be clear: you must at some point return to your agenda for the meeting. In extreme cases, where an irrelevant speaker will not let go of the floor, it may be necessary to ask for help from security personnel, but this step is as rare as it is radical. In most situations, the AARP method will satisfy the proponents of irrelevant ideas that you are taking them seriously.

Loaded Questions

Possibly a more difficult obstacle from a hostile audience, and one that requires even more skill to handle properly, is a loaded question coming from a member of the board or committee you are presenting to. In this case, usually because they are paying your bills (or you would like them to), sensitivities on both sides are heightened. Loaded questions usually come from a person who supports the hiring of a different design team, or who has an issue with the leadership of the board or committee, or who just likes to stir things up by asking provocative questions.

The loaded question is one for which there is no good answer, because the question contains in it an assumption of guilt. "Do you still beat your wife?" is the textbook example of a loaded question. An architectural example would be, "I heard your projects never come in on budget. Why is that?" Implicit in the question is the assumption that it must be true that your firm's work is always over budget.

When you are the target of a loaded question, it's fair to assume that you have a problem—with the questioner, if nothing else. As outlined above, there are a number of reasons why a panelist might ask such a question, some of which have nothing to do with you or your firm. So you must first assess what the motivation of the questioner is. If she is merely grandstanding to demonstrate to the panel or the audience or the cable television viewer that she is an astute guardian of the public treasury, you should by all means affirm her astuteness and compliment her on her diligence, while disabusing her of the untrue rumor she offered.

On the other hand, if you know beforehand that the question's purpose is to get you fired (or not hired), you should respond more succinctly, with a very brief rebuttal, and try to move the discussion in another direction. The last thing you want in a presentation is to give a declared enemy of your objective the floor for very long. Brevity, not defensiveness, is the best approach in this instance.

The third possibility, someone who just likes to stir things up by asking provocative questions, is more easily handled. Similar to the first example, if the questioner is just creating controversy because he likes to, compliment him effusively for his diligence and give a factual answer that defuses the

REMINDER

In dealing with loaded questions, it's critical to consider the motivation of the questioner.

bomb. What the pot-stirrer is looking for is camera time, a quote in the paper, or a sound bite, and as long as the record is set straight, there's no reason to deny it to him.

Overcoming Technical Problems

In any performance, there are bound to be technical problems. It is the rare play, musical, concert, or dance program that goes from start to finish with no technical glitches whatsoever. Light and sound cues are missed, the music starts too early or too late, scenery flies in or out too soon—the list of possible screwups is nearly endless. Architectural presentations, too, suffer from technical problems, some preventable, most not. The key is to take stock of the problem and, if at all possible, to keep going.

There are, in reality, very few technical problems that can completely ruin a presentation, particularly if you have done your homework ahead of time and understand reasonably well where the pitfalls may lie. But things will go wrong—depend on it. Overcoming technical obstacles is mostly the art of keeping your cool when the lights go off.

What kinds of technical problems can occur in a design presentation? Lights can burn out or go off inadvertently; sound systems can feed back or fail altogether; projectors (famously) can fail at the crucial moment; drawings can fall off the wall where they seemed securely taped only moments ago—as with arts performances, the list is nearly endless. If you stay in the profession long enough, you will get to experience each of these technical failures in turn—and many more besides.

Rather than deal with each problem and its solution individually, it would seem more useful to suggest some basic principles for dealing with them. One way to look at technical glitches is to perform a sort of intellectual triage on the disaster. Ask yourself the following questions, in this order:

> *Is this problem life-threatening?* If so, stop the show immediately. There is no reason to endanger any person so you can keep presenting.

> *Does this problem make it impossible to continue presenting?* An example would be a power failure in a windowless room. While not life-threatening, presenting in total darkness would be a difficult challenge, to say the least. In such a case, it would seem wise to address the problem before attempting to continue.

> *Can this problem be fixed quickly?* If all your sagging drawings need is the quick application of a couple pieces of tape, by all means keep the program rolling as you make the repair. One mistake many amateur presenters make is assuming that they must stop talking to make minor adjustments or repairs. In reality, very few technical obstacles fall under the first two headings above.

> *If the problem is too large to allow for a quick fix in real time, is it possible to fix within the time allotted for the presentation?* If so, think how your presentation might be adjusted to allow for the fix to take place. An example would be the projector lamp that needs replacement: this takes too long, usually, to accomplish on the fly, but if a spare lamp is available, it might well be accomplished by another team member while the presenter jumps ahead to the next topic—even questions and answers. Simply say that due to this technical problem, you're going to veer off your planned agenda briefly to see if you can get it

fixed and come back to this part of the presentation later.

It sounds breathtakingly easy, yet it's surprising how many presenters overlook these obvious strategies when things blow up during the nervous excitement of a live presentation. The main reason is that they naively expect that everything will go all right, and when things don't, they become rattled and behave irrationally, either stopping a presentation that can be salvaged or forging ahead when stopping would be a more appropriate response.

Overcoming Interaction

If you've followed the discussion to this point, you know that interaction is a good thing, not a bad thing, in presentations, so you might wonder why it needs to be overcome. In most cases, it doesn't: having lots of interaction with your audience means that they are engaged in what you are talking about. But it is possible, in rare cases, to have too much of a good thing, particularly if you have a chatty client group that knows each other well and likes to banter about irrelevant topics—kidding each other about their bad golf swings, for example. In such cases, you need a strategy for reducing the interaction so that you can return the focus to your objective for the presentation.

This can be difficult. Once you have opened the door for interaction to occur, it's not easy to close it without appearing to be a spoilsport. You need to regain control of the meeting without alienating the audience and without completely closing off the potential for future interaction. At such a point, it is all right to say something like, "I'm afraid we may be getting a little off track here. Perhaps I can draw us back to the main point of our discussion, which

TIP

If interaction gets out of hand (that is, off the subject), you need to regain control of the meeting without alienating the audience.

Lose Your Place?

You should never lose your place in a presentation. Losing your place implies one of several things, none of which are recommendations you'll find in this book:

▶ You are speaking from a manuscript.

▶ You are trying to give a memorized speech from a script.

▶ You are talking about a subject with which you lack familiarity.

▶ You are in the middle of a very long discourse during which there are no other speakers.

▶ You did not spend enough time preparing for the discussion.

As you can see from the list above, losing your place is not the problem; it is a symptom of a presentation that is planned incorrectly. But if you should lose your train of thought in a presentation, here's what to do:

▶ Smile. If possible, chuckle a bit as well. (Hey, we're all human, right?)

▶ Apologize for the interruption in the flow of your presentation.

▶ Consult your notes or outline, or ask someone where you are—preferably someone on your own team, but a member of the audience will do in a pinch.

▶ Proceed.

See the discussion in Chapter 8, "Be in the Moment," for some further thoughts on getting over your miscues and getting on with the presentation.

was...." While this may seem a risky approach—who wants to interrupt a group of people having a good time?—it is vastly preferable to losing control of the meeting entirely. You might even be appreciated as someone who can stay focused on the task at hand, even by an informal and collegial client group.

Overcoming Stage Fright

In some cases, the obstacle that most needs to be overcome is the reluctance of the presenter him- or herself. Stage fright is a common name for a paralyzing fear that can make even experienced professionals feel like blubbering idiots in front of an audience.

There are several facts to keep in mind in overcoming this all-too-common obstacle:

- *Stage fright is extremely common.* There is almost no one who speaks publicly who doesn't feel stage fright at some point in the presentation. Most of the audience can sympathize with the person who is on the spot, because they have had to make a presentation at some point, too.

- *Stage fright is a symptom of physical tension that has been left untreated.* A large portion of Chapter 1, "Show Up," is a discussion of how to use tension as part of your physical preparation to present. But understanding tension as a physical, not an emotional or intellectual, problem and using physical means to control it, is critical.

- *Stage fright is not a permanent condition.* Even the most frightened speaker will settle down eventually (although in extreme cases, not until his or her talk has concluded!). Recognizing stage fright as a normal—and temporary—phenomenon is the largest part of overcoming it.

- As was discussed in "The Practice Paradox" in Chapter 3, one of the most effective ways to combat stage fright is by becoming a more experienced speaker, not by practicing a specific speech over and over.

REMINDER

There is almost no one who speaks publicly who doesn't feel stage fright at some point in the presentation.

Summing It Up

Keeping going, one of the principal rules of show business, means that even if the curtains fall from the stage, the show should continue unless life or health is endangered. Your ability to overcome obstacles (or not) may tell the client more about you than what you had planned to say. There are a variety of obstacles any presenter will face if you stay at it long enough:

- *Expectable obstacles.* These are the things a prudent speaker plans for, even though you certainly don't want them to happen: late flights, equipment failure, missed shipments, ringing cell phones, blown fuses, and so on. You should have a contingency plan for each expectable obstacle.

- *Unexpected obstacles.* These are the wild cards, the things that even prudent presenters don't plan for. They include things like the audience not showing up (or leaving midway), building-wide power failure, or other emergencies. Your major decision, when faced with these unexpected roadblocks, is whether to continue with the presentation or attempt to reschedule it.

- *Audience hostility.* Sometimes when presenting to a hostile board or panel, you feel like a Christian being thrown to the lions. Use empathy and engagement (Chapter 5) to win over hostile audiences.

- *Inappropriate feedback.* Often a presentation will be interrupted by questions that are hostile or irrelevant. The AARP method (acknowledge, affirm, record, persevere) is the best way to handle those live grenades that are lobbed to you in the middle of a talk.

- *Technical problems.* Most technical glitches fall under the heading of "expectable obstacles." As discussed in Chapter 4, "Find Your Light," the key to overcoming technical problems is having a thorough understanding of the technical setup of your presentation and the room you are using. Architects seldom have the luxury of a technical director to manage lights and sound for them during a presentation.

► *Excessive interaction.* Bear in mind that interaction is generally a good thing; it is excessive only when it wanders entirely away from the subject of your presentation into fishing stories or discussions of current events. Curb excessive interaction by taking control of your agenda and steering the discussion back to the subject at hand.

► *Stage fright.* The paralyzing fear of speaking in public is more common than most people realize. Combat it by being physically ready to present (Chapter 1), giving all presenters a chance to speak early in the presentation (Chapter 2), and learning from experience that no matter how sweaty you are when you start talking, you'll eventually settle down.

Project

7

Often, an actor, rehearsing a play in a darkened theater, hears a direction yelled from the center of the auditorium: "Project!" This brief criticism means that the director can't hear what the actor is saying. And if the director, who usually is seated in the best seat in the house, can't hear, much of the (at that point hypothetical) audience won't be able to hear, either.

In the theater, there are many sins an actor can commit, but few are more annoying than the inability to project. In the not-long-ago days before sound reinforcement systems became commonplace, it was considered routine for a company of actors to fill theaters of two thousand seats or more with just the sound of their own voices, relying on little more than lung power and good acoustics. Today, theatricals from children's plays to Broadway productions rely on concealed wireless microphones and expensive sound systems to carry the story to the audience, but the well-trained actor still knows how to project.

What and How

What is projection? Simply stated, it is a way of speaking in order to be heard by many people, but doing so without shouting. Certainly, cheerleaders at a football game project, but yelling at the top of your lungs is not desirable for the small crowds that normally attend architectural briefings. Projection is filling a room with the sound of your voice, with or without electronic amplification.

Why is projecting important? Most architects, most of the time, are not required to fill an auditorium of over a thousand seats with their voice—although it's not as difficult as you might think. But projection involves two ideas that are critical for any presentation: first, making absolutely sure that everyone in the audience in any size or shape of room can hear you, and second, controlling the physical actions that make up your voice so that you can sound both confident and relaxed at the same time.

How does projection work? Actually, projection is as much about listening as it is about talking. You need to tune your ears to the space you are presenting in so that you can adjust the volume of your voice to be loud enough, but not too loud. We'll look at vocal modulation shortly. When you are projecting properly, you can hear yourself through sound that is reflected back to you from the rear of the room.

Projection also involves how you propel your voice out into the space. The physiology of projection will be discussed in the section below on "Breath Control." It's not difficult to understand, but it's also not something that most design professionals have heard much about.

Vocal Modulation

As mentioned above, the goal of projection is to fill the room, whatever its size, with the sound of your voice. In doing so, you must be careful not to overproject, which can come across as unnecessary shouting, pompousness, or simply too much energy for the room.

Your goal is to make yourself heard by the person farthest away in the audience. You will find that by speaking to the last person in the last row, in a voice that can easily be heard by that person, you will also be heard by every other person in the room. Conversely, if you speak only to those in the front row, even if they are the selection committee, people in back will be unable to hear you. So your vocal target, in any size or shape of room, is, conceptually, the "last row of the balcony." If the people in the cheap seats can hear you, so can the people in the expensive seats.

On the other hand, it is important not to overplay your part. You want to speak loudly enough to be heard by the person in the back row, but only just loud enough. This is where listening becomes important. Your voice, in most spaces, should come back to you sounding clear and undistorted. If you can't hear yourself at all, you're probably not projecting. If, on the other hand, you can hear yourself too well, with booming echoes and loud reverberations, you're probably overplaying the space. The sound check, discussed below, is a useful tool for understanding and managing projection.

REMINDER

Your goal is to make yourself heard by the farthest person in the audience.

Breath Control

One aspect of projection that makes it a challenge for nonprofessionals is that most people breathe without thinking about it. This is perfectly fine for most pursuits, like playing chess and working on a computer. But breathing is very important in performance art, and breath control is a crucial part of being able to support your voice so that you don't have to yell to fill the room with your voice.

Because breathing is involuntary, most people give it little thought, unless they have a breathing disorder. But from the point of view of presenting, most presenters have a breathing problem and don't know it. When you are asleep (i.e., completely relaxed), your breathing is controlled by a muscle between the lungs and the stomach called the diaphragm. The evidence of what is called "diaphragmatic breathing" can be seen by watching a sleeping child, where the stomach, not the chest, is what appears to move in and out with each breath.

Adults, on the other hand, when placed in stressful situations, often resort to a type of breathing called "chest breathing." Chest breathers self-consciously inflate their lungs as if they are getting ready to blow out the candles on a birthday cake. Evidence of chest breathing is obvious inflation of the rib cage, and rising and falling shoulders.

The problem with chest breathing is that, birthday cakes notwithstanding, it is inefficient. You are not getting as much oxygen in your lungs when you chest breathe as when you breathe diaphragmatically. As a consequence, your voice comes out sounding pinched and stressed, as opposed to relaxed and confident. In the same way, chest breathers have a difficult time projecting to the far corners of even a moderately large room. In fact, chest breathing can sometimes place such a burden on the speaker that he or she begins to hyperventilate or even pass out. This is the extreme example of the problem of inadequately supported breathing.

Fortunately, chest breathing can be overcome with practice. It's best to practice diaphragmatic breathing when you're not yet in the heat of a presentation: for example, the day before or on a cab ride to the meeting place. Simply sit still (or, if possible, lie down) and inhale deeply through your nose, taking care to use your stomach muscles for the intake and output of air. Notice how your abdomen rises and falls, and how easy it is to get a good helping of air with each breath. For contrast, if you like, try self-consciously inflating your lungs by expanding your chest, and see how ineffective that really is.

TIP

Remember to breathe from the diaphragm, not the chest.

Diaphragmatic breathing is very much a function of feeling relaxed—that's why even nervous people can do it while they're asleep. The problem is that few design professionals are relaxed in the moments before an interview. It's difficult to stay loose in those anxious moments before you "go onstage." Refer to Chapter 1 for reminders of how to stay physically warm and relaxed before a big presentation.

Breathing is another matter, however. If you don't think about it, your breathing will tend to rise to your chest, and you'll find yourself gasping for air. So even though in the moments before you speak you will definitely not feel very relaxed, do take a moment to check yourself for proper breathing. Remember to breathe from the diaphragm, not the chest, and continue to practice it for as long as you're not speaking. Eventually, you can train your body to breathe the right way when you're actually presenting.

Like the analogy of the golf lesson in the discussion of movement in Chapter 1, this focus on breathing may seem burdensome and distracting at first, especially if you are presenting to a group of four or six people where projection is a nonissue. But proper breathing is fundamental to public speaking, and while it may be difficult or even impossible to think about breathing while you are in the middle of a presentation, it's worth putting it on your "preflight" checklist for the minutes you are waiting to present.

Acoustical Considerations

Architects and designers are called to present in many different types of rooms, with many different types of acoustics. Without going into a long discussion of acoustics, most designers are aware that rooms can either have "live" (highly reflective) or "dead" (highly absorptive) acoustical characteristics. Fortunately, most rooms used for presenting are somewhere in between, with both reflective and absorptive materials. But if you do enough presentations, you will have the opportunity to speak in rooms that are as lively as a subway toilet and as dead as all outdoors. You need to vary your vocal approach to suit the circumstances.

Overly Live

It's easy to recognize spaces that are overly live: every scrape of a chair leg on the hard floor is amplified a hundred times by the hard walls and ceilings, so that each extraneous sound becomes a cacophony of noise. Echoes are frequently a problem in overly live rooms, and speech can actually be blurred by too many reflections reaching the listener's ear too close together.

As a speaker, it's important to limit your volume in an overly live space to the minimum threshold that will allow you to be heard. It's easy to get carried away in a live room, and sometimes the echoes have an oddly reassuring effect on a speaker, but it's easy to go too far. In a very live space, try to speak so that the person in the last row can hear you, but just barely. It won't be that difficult for that person, and it will keep you from blowing out the eardrums of the people up front.

Another problem with very live spaces is that the multiple sound-reflecting surfaces tend to blur speech. What works well for organ music works much less well for technical presentations. As a result, in an overly live space, you should slow down your delivery (even to the point of sacrificing energy) to ensure that everyone in the audience not only can hear, but also can understand, what you are saying.

Entirely Dead

Occasionally, you will have to present in a room with thick carpeting, heavy drapery, and a sound-absorbing ceiling, where there are no discernable echoes at all. The ultimate dead space is outdoors, where reflecting surfaces are nonexistent and ambient noise competes for the listeners' attention. Obviously, presenting outdoors is a unique challenge that should be avoided whenever possible. But there are rooms that approach the outdoors in their noise-reduction coefficient. How should you project in those rooms?

You will need to turn up the volume a bit in an overly dead space. That's because the person in the back row is unable to benefit from reflected sound bouncing off walls and ceilings, requiring you to provide the necessary amplitude by yourself. The challenge is to make yourself heard by the person in the farthest seat when you can hardly hear yourself. This is where the sound check comes in handy.

As you might expect, dead spaces provide a high level of speech accuracy—if the audience can hear you. So you needn't be as concerned with slow delivery or perfect diction as in an acoustically live environment.

Sound Check

If at all possible, do a sound check of the room you are presenting in. The earlier the better, of course, but even if you have a quick moment while you are setting up, "talk to the room" in the voice you plan to use for the presentation. Can you hear yourself clearly? Are the room acoustics very live or very dead? Will the person sitting in the corner be able to understand every word you say? Is there anything you can do to make the acoustics more suitable for your presentation? (Opening a curtain, for example, will add reflection to a space as the glass comes into play; just be sure you're not creating problems with daylight, as discussed in Chapter 4.) If you are using presentation boards, the boards can be arranged in such a way as to reinforce the sound of your voice for the audience—if you plan ahead.

Of course, show business professionals always do a sound check before a production. They know that even if the performers use the same mikes, the same speakers, and the same amplifiers as last night and the night before, different spaces will sound different based on the characteristics of the space. So they run through all the various facets of a program in the space to estimate how it will sound with a full house (and of course, it sounds different with a full house because bodies change the acoustical character of a space as well, usually making it much deader than it was empty).

If you are using sound reinforcement (microphones), the importance of a preperformance sound check is underscored. A clip-on mike can work much better or much worse by moving it an inch or so up or down your tie or blouse, which is not a discovery you necessarily want to make during your presentation. Or you may decide to dispense with microphones altogether, reasoning that neither the room nor the audience is large enough to warrant it. Just be sure to test everyone who will speak, all the mikes, and any other sound effects you may have brought. The one sound component you don't test will invariably be the one that doesn't work correctly.

TIP

If you will be using sound reinforcement (microphones), a preperformance sound check is especially important.

Using Microphones

Speaking of microphones, the design professions seem to be headed down the same path as the performing arts in their growing dependence on these devices. Presentations that used to be routine are now routinely recorded for posterity, and even the most mundane zoning hearing often involves the use of microphones, transcription, or cable television. How can you deal with one more piece of recalcitrant technology without completely losing track of the objective of your presentation?

The sound check, mentioned above, is a critical tool. You have to know ahead of time where the mikes are, how they get used, and what options you have. Often, a wireless or handheld mike can be made available to you if you simply ask for it. What is inexcusable is finding yourself tethered to a miked podium because you were unwilling or too late to ask whether other options might be available.

Microphones are sensitive tools—especially the tiny clip-on variety—and inexperienced speakers never seem to know how to hold—or where to clip—them. Positioning a microphone too close to your mouth will result in a booming, distorted sound that will annoy your listeners. Holding or clipping it too far from your mouth will prevent the mike from doing its job. Because every room and sound system is different, conducting a sound check is the only way to keep yourself from looking foolish using a microphone. Try different mike positions until you get a natural sound from the speakers in the room. Once you have found a mike position that works, lock it in by marking your tie or blouse or by taking careful note of where you are holding the microphone. Then try to keep to that position throughout your talk.

You may have noticed that professional singers pull the mike away from themselves when they sing especially loudly. Or you may have seen a lounge singer almost swallow a microphone during a soft passage in a song. Professional singers know how to use the mike position to get more (or less) out of their vocal performance. For the most part, this is not a skill many architects need to learn—unless your presentations include particularly loud or quiet passages. The point is that, with a handheld mike, you can vary the position to compensate for variety in the loudness of your presentation.

You'll recall from the discussion of appropriate movement in Chapter 1 that the lectern is your worst enemy in terms of providing an engaging, animated presentation. So your choice of microphones, should you have any, should be in the following order:

1. Clip-on wireless mike (often called a lavaliere)
2. Handheld wireless mike (major drawback: one less hand to work with)

3. Clip-on or handheld corded mike (one more thing to trip over)

4. Floor mike (at least they can see you!)

5. Fixed-podium mike (inability to move becomes your major disadvantage)

6. Fixed-tabletop mike (even worse—you're stuck in one place *and* you're sitting down!)

On the rare occasion when you are called to give testimony before Congress, you will be stuck with the least desirable microphone option and very little you can do about it. This is unfortunate, but not necessarily fatal to your objective. Just plan ahead on how you will get sufficient movement, animation, and energy into a presentation where you might as well be strapped to your chair. (Hint: You may have to dial up the pitch and/or pace of your talk to keep the same energy level.)

Should an architect ever bring a sound system (with microphones) with him or her to a presentation? Unless the presentation is outdoors, no. Most design presentations are to small enough groups that miking is totally unnecessary. It's an historical fact that eighteenth-century Protestant revivalist George Whitefield routinely preached in the open air to crowds exceeding ten thousand. If George could do that, surely you can present to a meeting room with fifty or sixty people in it without using a microphone!

Summing It Up

Projection is simply the art of filling the room with the sound of your voice, so that the person in the worst seat in the house can hear you easily. If that person can hear, then so can everyone else.

- You need to modulate your voice so as to fill a large room (this may require additional support) or to not overpower a small room (this may require you to back off a little). In either case, your target is still that person in the last row.
- Practice diaphragmatic breathing to achieve adequate projection, particularly in larger rooms. When you are breathing with your diaphragm, your stomach is moving more than your chest or shoulders.
- In rooms with very lively acoustics, you need to talk much less loudly to be heard by that person in the last row. But you also need to speak more slowly and clearly to overcome muddying reflections.
- In rooms that are acoustically dead, you will need more projection to achieve the same audibility as in a room with more moderate acoustical properties.
- Doing a sound check in advance of the presentation is a good way to understand how a space will behave and how much you need to project.
- Microphones are becoming increasingly common in public presentations, although they are unnecessary for most groups. When you have a choice in the matter, ask for a mike that doesn't limit your ability to move around and engage the audience.

Be in the Moment

8

"I can't tell you how many times I've stepped on a dog's tail and the dog just looks up and starts wagging it again. They live right in the moment, and they're on to the next thing."

—DAN DYE
owner, Three Dog Bakery

Until now, most of the "commandments of show business" have concerned relatively mundane—perhaps even obvious—rules of the stage. This chapter will take us a little deeper into the world of performance art, to a place where great performances are created by great artists every time they take the stage. That place is called "in the moment."

"In the moment" is a phrase you hear in connection with performing arts, psychology, and occasionally with sports, usually in the form of a counterpart phrase, "in the zone." It refers to a level of focus and concentration that most people, in their everyday lives, seldom aspire to or attain. But being in the moment is absolutely critical to delivering a successful presentation and accomplishing your objective. It requires you to devote 100 percent of your resources—physical, emotional, mental—to the task at hand, which is presenting. It's not enough to call it commitment, because commitment can be expressed in a variety of ways. A person who spends ninety hours a week at work is said to be committed, but how much of that time does he or she spend surfing the Internet or passing the time with coworkers? Being in the moment is a different level of commitment, the total commitment of self to a task or activity.

This may strike you as a little bizarre. It is not necessary to commit 100 percent of yourself to a presentation 100 percent of the time. Everyone has commitments that extend far beyond giving presentations. The key to being in the moment is the ability to temporarily set aside those other commitments while giving the presentation, so that your full energy can be devoted to the subject at hand. Before and after the presentation, you can still be an architect, project manager, parent, soccer coach, friend, spouse, or tai chi master. But being in the moment requires you to leave all those other roles at the door when you enter the venue for your presentation.

Part of being in the moment is the recognition that every design professional wears many hats and plays many roles, of which being a design professional is only one. We are not as single-minded as our resumes and our performance reviews would have us (and others) believe. We are enormously complex creatures with amazing abilities to think about more than one thing at a time. There is nothing wrong with having more than one thing going on in your head most of the time—don't most of the people in your office listen to music while they

RULE OF THUMB

Being in the moment is the ability to temporarily set aside other commitments while giving the presentation, so that your full energy can be devoted to the subject at hand.

design? The only time it is wrong to be multitasking is when you are presenting.

Why is this the case? An obvious theme of this book is that presentation is a performance art, just as much as dance, music, and theater—even basketball—are performing arts. Performing arts are different from everyday work in that they require a level of concentration and focus much higher than what most people do at work every day. It's not hard to understand (though it may be annoying) the counterperson at a convenience store talking on the telephone while scanning your candy bar. It would be much more difficult to imagine a concert violinist stopping in the middle of a piece to take a personal call. The performing arts demand more from the artist, at least during the time of the performance.

Unfortunately, many architects and designers have not gotten that message. They turn their cell phone ringers to the "vibrate" position so that the ringing won't annoy clients, but some still feel the need to take calls in a presentation setting. Nonspeakers do engineering calculations, check their personal organizers, or daydream when others are speaking. Even speakers sometimes allow their minds to wander, while they are speaking, to upcoming meetings, tasks, or vacations. Being in the moment may seem arcane to most technical professionals, but it is absolutely central to successfully conveying your message to your audience.

There are two main obstacles to being in the moment: the past and the future. The moment, of course, is right now, and being in the moment means bringing your full personality to bear on the activity taking place this second, whether you are speaking or not.

Forget the Past

The past can play havoc with presentations in a couple of ways: Some presenters are hampered with issues (baggage) that arise from painful past experiences; other presenters let a minor glitch encountered moments ago keep them from completing a presentation well. Both distant and recent past can spell trouble for presenters who are unable to remain in the moment.

Baggage Handling

The distant past holds presenters back by creating emotional encumbrances. You may be hampered in your presentation by thoughts of past presentations that did not go well, past clients who seemed hostile to your message, or simply recent events that have left you in a sour mood. All of these occurrences constitute the "baggage" you bring to a presentation. And like real baggage, this psychic baggage can leave you burdened, awkward, clumsy, and overexerted.

Some baggage may be very old. You may have been told, even as a child, that public speaking was not your strong suit, that you were boring, or that no one cared what you had to say. While it may take years of therapy to rid yourself permanently of such baggage, be assured that it is relatively simple to leave it outside the presentation room, at least for a while. All that is required is the recognition that this audience (as is most likely the case) doesn't know you that well, doesn't have many well-formed opinions about you, and isn't aware of what your third-grade teacher wrote on your "permanent record." Most often, audiences react in real time to what they see and hear, not to what someone told them about you. Long-ago baggage creates unnecessary self-consciousness by causing you to recall lots of things your audience is most likely unaware of and not likely to care much about anyway.

Getting rid of more recent baggage can be another chore altogether. If you have done a presentation in the past week or so that you feel didn't go well, some residue of that experience is bound to color your current challenge. Actors, as well as athletes, face this challenge when a new performance follows close on the heels of a bad one. Being in the moment demands that the performer (or presenter) leave the recent past behind to focus on the task at hand, the issue of the moment, the challenge of the day. The only benefit to be gained from reflecting on recent poor performances is in learning which mistakes not to repeat. This is a useful exercise for the preparation and rehearsal period, but not for the presentation itself. As far too many comedies have demonstrated, the best way to drop the cake is to keep reminding yourself, "Don't drop the cake."

A third type of baggage, and maybe the most difficult to deal with during a presentation, is the gaffe that occurs during the presentation itself. When an actor blows a line, misses an entrance or drops a cue, like all humans, she will become flustered. Her heart will race, she may blush, and her breathing may even become quick and shallow. But a professional actor will overcome those reactions more quickly than an amateur, by remaining "in the moment." That means that rather than berating herself in an interior monologue—"I can't believe I did that! How could I be so stupid?"—she simply picks up the thread of the action taking place onstage, and accepts that the director will make a note to give her the next day reminding her not to screw up. Professionalism is the ability to overcome minor (and major) mistakes in a performance without completely breaking the illusion the drama is intended to create.

The parallels to technical presentations should be fairly obvious. Although presenting your firm or your work shouldn't be an illusion, there is a flow to presentations that mistakes can interrupt. What is crucial is that you not allow yourself to be interrupted by minor mishaps and thus lose your concentration. Being in the moment will help you to stay focused on the goal of your presentation.

If you've ever watched a track meet, perhaps you've noticed that hurdlers don't lose points for hitting the hurdles. It may slow them down a fraction of a second, but it's theoretically possible to knock down every hurdle and still win the race. This is an apt metaphor for presenting. If you stay focused on your objective, it is possible—in theory at least—to make a mistake every two minutes during a twenty-minute presentation and still accomplish your objective, and maybe even win the commission. Because presenting is a dance, your ultimate success depends not on whether you miss a step or two, but on your ability to recover and keep smiling when you do it. It may be that you will be the only one who even knows that a step was missed.

Forget the Future

Because we live our lives forward, the past is usually a much larger obstacle to being in the moment than the future. But that doesn't mean that anticipation of future events doesn't affect your ability to be in the moment.

Anticipation is just as much the enemy of successful presenting as retrospection. Because anyone

TIP

It is crucial that you do not allow yourself to be interrupted by minor mishaps and thus lose your concentration.

RULE OF THUMB

Because presenting is a dance, your ultimate success depends not on whether you miss a step or two, but on your ability to recover and keep smiling when you do it.

Be in the Moment

can think faster than he or she can talk, speakers tend to think ahead to upcoming points or actions that must be taken. Under normal circumstances, this is not a problem. As long as things are going according to plan, thinking ahead may not create serious difficulties. But when you are living in the future, when your brain is racing ahead of the words you are saying, you are living as dangerously as a person driving while looking through a telescope. You may see a part of the road ahead and miss the pitfalls in your immediate vicinity.

In the theater, this habit of thinking ahead is called "anticipating," and it creates all kinds of problems. At a practical level, anticipating makes you "step on" other actors' lines, because you are so focused on what you are going to say that you fail to let them finish saying what they are supposed to say. At another level, anticipating bleeds the honesty out of a performance and makes it less about the action taking place onstage than about actors saying their lines to each other. Anticipating is deadly to dramatic action, and can make even an opening-night performance seem stale and overrehearsed.

Design professionals can also anticipate, by jumping up in the middle of someone else's talk to begin their own spiel. Or by obsessing about whether the video player is cued up for the exciting video that's been planned for the end of the presentation. Or by skipping ahead in their own agenda to points they had intended to cover later.

Being in the moment is the best cure for the curse of anticipation. If you make a concerted effort to be focused on what is being said at that moment, whether you are speaking or someone else is, you will have the best insurance possible against sins of anticipation. And your presentation will seem fresher and more spontaneous to the audience as well.

Planning, Not Thinking, Ahead

Presenting is not chess. Chess players are rewarded for anticipating their opponent's next four, eight, or ten moves. And to the extent that you can plan for a variety of possible eventualities and contingencies in your presentations, you will be rewarded. But presenting requires you to be lighter on your feet than a chess player, to make decisions in real time, and to react to what others are saying in real time. That is the essence of being in the moment.

You might ask the question, "Didn't you say to overprepare for a presentation, to have more information than you could possibly present? Aren't all those things anticipation?" Indeed, to deliver a good presentation requires a tremendous amount of planning and preparation, as has been emphasized repeatedly. But planning ahead before a presentation and thinking ahead during a presentation are two entirely different activities. There is every reason to plan ahead, to make careful and meticulous advance decisions about where everyone will sit, stand, talk, walk, and point. By the same token, there is every reason not to think ahead *when the presentation is taking place.* You will be caught off-guard, become tongue-tied or flustered, or even be stopped cold if you allow your thoughts to wander away more than an instant from what is going on right now in a presentation. Your fate will be the same as a second baseman thinking about his next at-bat when a grounder goes whistling between his legs.

REMINDER

Don't look too far ahead when you're presenting: You may see a part of the road ahead and miss the pitfalls in your immediate vicinity.

Be in the Moment

Listening

Another related obstacle to being in the moment is our inability to listen to what others are saying. This inability, which is chronic in the design professions, is a critical problem in presentations. Listening is an important component of being in the moment, because it connects you to what is going on around you.

Have you ever seen a presenter who was so intent on delivering his message that no one could get his attention to tell him that he was out of time, that his fly was open, that the slide projector had gone off? The inability to listen is symptomatic of not being in the moment. Even while you're talking, you must be able to hear and react to what is going on around you.

Listening will make you a better speaker. As you become able to transition from the lofty position of lecturer to a person engaged in a dialogue with an audience, you will find yourself more appreciated, more respected, and ironically, more highly regarded than the isolated dispenser of information.

TIP
Listening is an important component of being in the moment, because it connects you to what is going on around you.

TIP
Becoming a better listener will make you a better speaker.

What "In the Moment" Really Means

It is very difficult for human beings to live in the moment. Our brains are so capable of thinking ahead, and our memories are so vast, that the very idea of emptying out our storehouse of experiences for a few minutes of a presentation may strike you as ludicrous. But it is this almost animalistic ability to leave consideration of the past and the future for another time that marks the successful performance artist, and by implication, the successful presenter.

Part of the problem is that architects and designers don't practice in real time. Ours is a contemplative profession, where a problem is carefully (sometimes agonizingly carefully) stated, and a solution is crafted over a period of days, weeks, months, or years. Unlike the doctors on *E.R.*, we seldom have to make instantaneous decisions that affect the outcome of our work. Even "hot" issues in the field are resolved in hours or days, not instantly. This perspective works against us in presenting, because presenting truly is a form of performance art. It is never the same twice; it is affected by the viewer as much as by the presenter; and it takes place at a specific place and time, never to be reproduced. It is this real-time aspect of presenting that is most difficult for design professionals to grasp, because it is outside most of our professional experience.

But that is what being in the moment is all about. It is acknowledging (or pretending) that there is nothing in your world at this moment besides this presentation, and focusing all the intellect and energy you are capable of bringing to bear on this one particular moment in time. It is not all that difficult to check your issues at the door once you realize that presenting is not like the rest of your practice, that you don't multitask during presentations, that you need to listen to what others are saying, and that as far as this presentation is concerned, there is no yesterday and no tomorrow.

Summing It Up

Being in the moment means being 100 percent committed, body and soul, to the presentation at the time it is taking place. This requires a level of concentra-

Be in the Moment

tion and focus that is common to performance artists and athletes, but uncharacteristic of busy professionals.

- ▶ Being in the moment is, like showing up, first of all a physical phenomenon. It means bringing all of your personal resources to bear on the presentation.

- ▶ Unlike design, presenting is not a contemplative art. It takes place in real time, and requires your real involvement.

- ▶ Reflection may be a good quality to cultivate in your life in general, but it is fatal to presenting. You need to let go of past mistakes, both distant and recent, to focus on the present moment.

- ▶ Anticipation of upcoming events is equally dangerous. Anticipating means looking too far ahead, not reacting to things as they happen, and can result in your being seriously derailed by minor mishaps.

- ▶ Being in the moment sounds like pop psychology or advice from a self-help seminar, but it can make the difference between tired, stale presentations and lively, dynamic discussions.

Remember Your Props

9

Some years ago at a university symposium on design, three well-known architects were asked to talk about their design process without giving a slide presentation of their work. Not one of the invited speakers did as they were asked. All three used extensive slide presentations to talk about their work, leaving many in the audience wondering if the purpose of the symposium had been adequately explained to the speakers.

You might conclude from this anecdote that architects are congenitally unable to talk about their work without visual aids. We can imagine hearing a lecturer deliver a paper on nuclear physics or cancer treatments or social psychology without so much as a single chart, but for an architect to speak for more than two minutes without an image to point to is almost unthinkable.

RULE OF THUMB

Recognize that it is nearly impossible for a design professional to give a talk without visual aids.

Visual aids are not in and of themselves good or bad. Like most inanimate objects, they can be helpful or unhelpful depending on how they are used. Design professionals, strangely, have codified many of these unhelpful strategies into standard practice. This chapter will explore the variety of ways visual aids can be used to help your presentation, and some pitfalls to avoid.

Ownership Issues

The title of this chapter, "Remember Your Props," requires some explaining. One of the rules of show business that is embedded in this heading is the notion that it is the actor who bears the ultimate responsibility for his or her props making it on stage at the right time. "Prop" is short for *property*, which is stage jargon for any object that is used by actors in a play or movie (as opposed to *scenery*, which forms the background but is not directly involved in the action). Even if there are a number of stage managers, assistants, and property handlers assigned to a production, it is ultimately the actor's responsibility to ensure that his or her props are positioned properly for their ultimate use.

REMINDER

It is ultimately the presenter's responsibility to ensure that his or her props are positioned properly for their ultimate use.

The connection to presenting should be obvious: No matter how many graphic artists, outside contractors, A/V coordinators, and CAD technicians are involved in the creation and setup of your presentation, ultimate responsibility for props rests with the presenter. This is not just a sweeping generalization that corresponds to an architect placing his or her seal on drawings prepared by persons in his or her employ. It means that each presenter must personally verify that he or she has the necessary tools and supporting materials, and the means of getting all of it in and out of the presentation room. Others may assist, of course, but they can only assist—the responsibility for the presentation rests with the presenter.

Remember Your Props

Relating to Your Visuals

Another all-too-common problem with visual aids is how you interact with them. Commandment number 5, you will recall, is "Face Out," or the well-known alternative version, "Never turn your back on the audience." Often, architects become so enamored with their own drawings that they end up talking to the drawings instead of to the audience.

An obvious question this admonition raises is, "How can I face out when my drawings are facing the audience as well? Either I can see the drawings or I can see the audience, but I can't be looking at both."

There are a couple of strategies to employ in this regard. First, use the stage technique of "cheating out," which was discussed briefly in Chapter 5. Have you ever noticed when watching a play or a TV show filmed in front of a live audience that the actors almost never face each other directly? This is the principle of cheating out. Think of the presentation as a three-way conversation involving you, your visual aids, and the audience. In a three-way conversation, each participant stands at the vertex of a triangle, with the other two parties within roughly a 60-degree angle of vision (see Figure 9.1). Try to set up your room as though it were a three-way conversation where you and your audience are two participants and your visual aid is the third. If you do this, then you can see the audience and your visuals in the same cone of vision; the same goes for the other two corners of the triangle.

A second approach, one that is even more effective, is the TV weathercaster approach (see Figure 9.2). Have you ever noticed how television forecasters are able to stare into the camera while indicating weather facts on maps that are behind them? They're

WARNING

Often, architects become so enamored with their own drawings that they end up talking to the drawings instead of to the audience.

RULE OF THUMB

Think of the presentation as a three-way conversation involving you, your visual aids, and the audience.

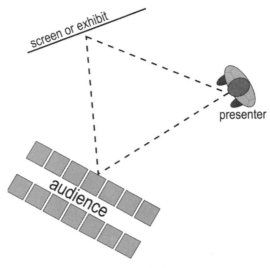

Figure 9.1

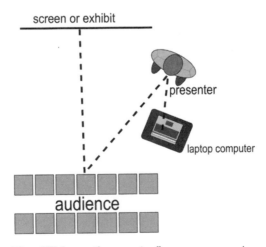

The "TV weathercaster" arrangement

Figure 9.2

Remember Your Props

not psychic; they simply have video monitors in front of them that show how they appear in front of the map. (In fact, they're not standing in front of a real map at all, just a blue screen that allows people in the control room to superimpose the meteorologist's image on a map). Presenters can do the same thing, though usually without the blue screen. Laptop computers linked to a projector allow you to "monitor" what's on the screen behind you—just like a TV weathercaster does. You'd be amazed at how rarely you need to turn and point at the screen when you and your audience are looking at each other.

What about Leave-behinds?

The leave-behind, a bound summary of a presentation or a supplement to a qualifications submittal, is a time-honored tradition in the design profession. So prevalent are leave-behinds in the profession that a competitor who fails to bring one to an interview runs the risk of being thought negligent or uninterested.

But leave-behinds are actually of very limited value. A municipal official whose job requires her to preside over numerous selection processes confided that, after a presentation, leave-behind booklets are almost never consulted by the selection panel, whose members may even resent receiving another stack of booklets in addition to the already voluminous stack of literature they have had to wade through to create a shortlist. Her advice is to forget the leave-behind booklet altogether, or if you must, create a "leave-ahead" handout that will allow the panel to follow along with your presentation, make notes on important points, and scrutinize your claims of flawless performance.

The traditional argument against leave-aheads is that people thumb through them during your presentation, skip ahead, jump to the bottom line (if there is a fee proposal involved), and otherwise use them to disrupt the flow of the presentation. This argument is worthy of consideration, but it was the opinion of the city official, who has seen enough presentations to know, that a leave-ahead is the only worthwhile handout to bring to an interview. A leave-behind booklet, in her view, is just so much wasted paper.

A related problem is architects' insistence on the fidelity of the projected image above all other considerations. In Chapter 4, "Find Your Light," the importance of a presenter finding his or her light and staying lit is emphasized. This obviously has implications for the fidelity of projected images. In general, it is preferable to let projected images suffer—a little—to ensure that the speaker is adequately lit. Though it is possible to have a speaker so well lit that projected images are unreadable, most architects err in the opposite direction, making rooms so dark that it is the speaker, not the image, that is invisible.

Visual Aids Overview

In this section, each of the most popular forms of visual aids for designers will be discussed as to its advantages and disadvantages. The point of this discussion is not to say with certainty that any one method is the best. Each presentation has its unique circumstances, content, and constraints. The purpose here is to help you make thoughtful decisions about which medium will help you achieve your objective for a given presentation. In other words, you should never use glossy presentation boards when a cocktail napkin will do the job—and vice versa.

This discussion will generally flow from older, tried-and-true visuals to newer technologies. Unlike the discussion of presentation formats, however, there is no hidden agenda here—the preferred medium is the one that works best for the presentation at hand. In general, the list ranges from older, more familiar technologies to newer ones, but the order of listing is not an indication of preference.

Presentation Boards

By far the oldest visual aids are drawings and other graphics mounted to presentation boards. Except for the models that were used to design, present, and construct the cathedrals, no presentation medium has been around longer. And despite the profession's increasing reliance on digital media, boards still play a major role in many presentations, because they have several advantages.

The primary advantage of presentation boards is their reality—once created, boards *exist*, and can be counted on to be available to the presenter without too much effort in the way of setup. This advantage may seem trivial, but to anyone who has ever had an equipment failure eliminate an electronic presentation at a critical time, it is definitely not a minor point. As reliable as they are, however, boards can still fail technically: they can warp, break, become dog-eared or delaminated. So boards must be treated tenderly to survive even one trip to a client's site.

Another advantage of boards is that, because they exist as individual entities, you can jump from one image to another fairly easily and in any sequence you choose. This puts the presenter using boards at an advantage over most users of computerized presentation software (with an exception that will be discussed later). This flexibility allows you to interact more with your audience. Finally, because they are not a projected medium, boards allow you to leave the lights on at full brightness throughout your presentation, an obvious plus.

Presentation boards have a few other disadvantages. For one, they are expensive to produce, requiring both plotter time (usually in color nowadays) and dry-mounting, which can easily run $50 per board or more. For more than a few boards, these costs adds up quickly for a visual that, more often than not, is used once and then placed in a storage room until it is discarded.

Another limitation of boards is their size. Presentation boards trade off portability for visibility—that is, the smaller they are, the less able they are to be seen. Conversely, really large boards are easy to read but exceedingly difficult to transport. A related problem is the complexity of dealing with multiple presentation boards at one time. Any presentation with more than about twelve presentation boards is likely to become a card-shuffling comedy of errors as you struggle to keep the right visuals on the right easels at the right time. Easels themselves are a frequent bugaboo. You have to bring your own or carelessly trust in the suitability of those the client might (or might not) have on hand.

Overheads

One of architects' least-used presentation technologies, at least until the past few years, has been overhead projection. There are two types of overhead projection used for presentations: one a time-tested and almost quaint technology, the other high-tech and contemporary. Each will be looked at briefly in this section.

Traditional Overheads

You can probably count on one hand the number of architectural presentations you have seen using the traditional overhead projector and loose transparencies (also called "foils"). When the business world adopted the overhead as the standard form of communication a generation ago, architects all but ignored it.

There are reasons for this medium's low level of acceptance in the design professions. Many traditional overhead projectors project an unevenly lit, distorted image that architects considered unacceptable for rendering plans or photographs of built work. This limitation alone served to sink the traditional overhead in the minds of most design professionals. But much design work consists of elements other than plans and photos: many meetings consist largely of going over program information or budgets or schedules, and for these, overhead projection works well. Traditional overheads combine the flexibility (and reality) of boards with a medium that is easy to transport, reliable, and inexpensive. Overheads are cheap to produce, highly readable, and don't require room lights to be dimmed in most situations. Another advantage is that overhead projectors spill a lot of light onto the presenter (you), which makes you easy to see, even if someone does decide to dim the room lights.

The primary disadvantage of traditional overheads has been mentioned already—the medium doesn't do justice to photographs or renderings. So you probably would not choose to use overheads in a marketing presentation where your work really has to shine. On the other hand, the familiarity and casual nature of overheads can make your presentation less intimidating than using giant boards or more advanced technology.

Computer Overheads

In contrast to traditional overhead foils, computer overhead projection is taking over the business world and the design professions at an almost equal pace. Typically, this technology consists of an LCD projector driven by a laptop computer using some form of presentation software. So pervasive is this medium that an Appendix is given over to the discussion of how to use presentation software to your best advantage. For now, let's consider the pros and cons of computer overheads versus other types of visual aids.

For a profession as steeped in tradition as architecture, computer overhead presentations have caught on surprisingly fast. Although not as prevalent as in, say, the Defense Department, laptop-driven presentations have become increasingly common for architects in the past decade. There are a number of reasons for this acceptance, but the primary one is that the projection technology has caught up in quality to the venerable slide projector. A good-quality LCD projector can now produce an image that is indistinguishable from a slide, and can in some cases be better. LCD projectors are still relatively expensive, but as with all electronics, prices fall and quality increases with amazing rapidity.

What are the advantages of a computer-driven presentation? First on many lists would be their versatility. Because these presentations are "virtual" in the sense that there doesn't need to be any physical artifact—not even a slide—presenters can change the content or the order of the presentation up until the moment they start presenting. Since architects as a group love to fuss with things until the eleventh (or twelfth) hour, this is a huge advantage. Computer presentations can also help you add structure to your presentation by putting your outline on the screen for you and the audience to follow (this can also be done with slides, but requires considerably more advance planning to carry out). And presentation

TIP

Since computer overhead presentations are "virtual," presenters can change the content or the order of the presentation up until the moment they start presenting.

software allows you to easily add titles and other graphic elements to your presentation.

Other advantages of computer overheads include their negligible cost; once you have bitten the bullet of acquiring a rather expensive projector that will be obsolete in eighteen months, it costs almost nothing to create a presentation with five, fifty, or five hundred images, except for the time required to assemble it. (Associated with this fact is the risk of overloading a presentation with more "slides" than time allows.) Still another advantage is the ability to incorporate a variety of media (photographs, drawings, renderings, video, even music) in a single file, which can be run automatically or by pushing the Page Down key on your computer. And contrary to what you might think, computer-driven LCD projectors can be a "lights-on" presentation technique. They don't work outdoors in daylight, but they can create a good image at short range, even in well-lit rooms.

The primary disadvantage of computer-driven overhead projection is that it involves technology, which makes some presenters nervous—with good reason. Even the most seasoned presenter will at one time or another be faced with a balky laptop, a recalcitrant projector, or two seemingly good pieces of equipment that simply refuse to "talk." The importance of a backup plan (see Chapter 6, "Keep Going") cannot be overstated. Also, computer slide shows are usually linear—that is, one image following another in sequence—making it difficult to improvise or change the agenda to suit the audience. It can be done, however; how to do it is explained in the Appendix. And the "virtuality" of computer projection leaves some presenters (and their audiences) cold, as there are often no paper drawings or models with which to interact.

Models

Arguably the oldest of all presentation media, presentation models have long been a favorite of architects for communicating design ideas. Their primary advantage is that they communicate three-dimensional ideas in three dimensions (which not even so-called 3-D computer images do). There is often no substitute for showing a client a design idea in the proportions you actually intend the project to take.

The principal advantage of models is also a shortcoming, however. Because they are not full-size, clients tend not to fully appreciate the experiential qualities of a project, even through the medium of a model. Similarly, models tend to give clients an aerial perspective, appropriate for understanding form and massing of a project, but not always its inner workings. And because they involve a level of abstraction, models at times seem much more real to their designers than they to do clients who may view them as assemblages of plastic and mat board.

Models are, of course, expensive and difficult to create, and as such, tend to impart a preciousness to design ideas that may be inappropriate for early stages of the design process. But they do create a stir when brought into a room, and their toylike quality and charm may, in the final analysis, be the best argument in their favor.

Video and Computer Animation

Nowadays, the phrase "building a model" often refers not to a cardboard mockup but to a three-dimensional representation of a project created in

TIP

The primary advantage of models is that they communicate three-dimensional ideas in three dimensions.

cyberspace, and viewed either as a series of static views (called renderings, although they bear little resemblance to the painted renderings of old) or as an animated series of views, called an animation or a video. Architects have moved beyond the "gee-whiz" period of computer animation—when the fact that it could be done was reason enough to do it—and have begun to seriously consider how computer modeling can help explain design ideas to a client or user group. At the same time, rendering and animation software have continued to improve, so that even small firms have the ability to create polished animations.

TIP

The advantages of computer animations are still mostly contained in their ability to dazzle.

The advantages of computer animations are still mostly contained in their ability to dazzle. Because of the time required to render each frame (an interval that gets smaller with each successive generation of microprocessors), animations tend to move quickly around and through a project, giving a good sense of the overall, but without much ability to stop and consider the particulars. On the other hand, computer models have an advantage over physical models in that they allow the user to experience the project at eye level, as a real person would, not just flying above it in a helicopter.

The main disadvantage of computer animation and video is, like physical models, the time and expense required to produce them—one difference being that the virtual model often becomes the basis of the project documentation. And making a good animation requires tremendous amounts of computer time, which, even though automated, can push completion of these projects dangerously close to presentation deadlines. Producing a real video requires yet another layer of production to add visual effects, graphics, and sound to create a truly polished presentation piece.

But perhaps the biggest limitation of computer models and animations is the one identified by media theorist Marshall McLuhan: television (and by implication, video, animated video, and computer-generated video) is a "cool" medium, meaning that it's a low-involvement form of communication that asks very little of its audience. As such, even the best video presentation has the effect of cooling off an audience, disengaging them from the reality of the presentation. Presenting is like live theater; video is like watching TV. There is a palpable difference in the level of audience engagement and response. The worst possible use of video—one that is strongly not recommended—is to show a promotional video during your presentation, during which a narrator says things about you or your firm that you could be say-

Choose Your Weapon

The most important factor in your choice of visual aids is to choose the ones that will help you achieve your objective. At times, your choice will be constrained by circumstances (a day-lit room, say, or a client who abhors PowerPoint and tells you so). More often, the choice of visual aids is yours. First, consider all the options that are available to you. Review the discussion above if necessary. Second, consider which media will be most effective in conveying the message you want to convey to your audience. As Marshall McLuhan pointedly observed, to some degree, "the medium is the message." But see the sidebar titled "The Inversion Principle": sometimes technology has the reverse of the effect you intend. Finally, and no less importantly, choose a presentation medium that you are personally comfortable with. No audience wants to hear a presenter utter the words, "Well, I've never used one of these before, so wish me luck." If it's absolutely critical to your objective to use a technology with which you are uncomfortable and unfamiliar, the time to get comfortable and familiar with it is before, not during, the presentation.

Remember Your Props

ing live. This sort of "commercial" is the surest way to disengage an already skeptical audience.

The Best Visual Aids

At the other end of the spectrum from the carefully crafted project video is the place where architects and designers really have a chance to shine in the presentation room. The best visual aids are the ones that are created on the spot, on the spur of the moment, driven by the architect's innate need to communicate visually. These can be as simple as words on a flip chart (where the audience can admire the neat lettering you learned in school), a diagram on a marker board, or a bold slash across a drawing or a presentation board. (Not surprisingly, the most difficult place to make instant graphics is on the screen of your laptop computer.) But these instant visuals help to remind audiences that they are not listening to an accountant or economic consultant, but to a creative professional who is self-selected and trained to think visually. Sometimes the most carefully crafted presentations do a disservice when the presenter becomes so distant from the content that he or she could just as easily be a hired talker as an architect or designer. One way to break down that barrier is to create graphics in the room, in real time, in front of the audience.

 TIP

The best visual aids are created on the spot, driven by the architect's innate need to communicate visually.

Despite our comfort with the graphical tools—pens and markers—architects are at times reluctant to take advantage of this powerful medium, one that helps to differentiate them from other professionals, as well as from competitors. Much of this reluctance stems from insecurity with presenting as performance art—as part of what architects actually do—and the tendency to view a presentation as an unnat-

The Inversion Principle

Because visual aids run the gamut from crude markings to highly polished computer-aided design work, you might tend to think that the more sophisticated an audience is, the more they expect to see the latter and resent the former. Although no scientific studies exist to support this theory, the Inversion Principle holds the opposite to be the case: In general, the less sophisticated the audience, the more they will be amazed by high-tech wizardry, either a laptop-driven presentation or a computer-generated fly-through. Conversely, and perhaps more controversially, the Inversion Principle holds that a more sophisticated client, being fully aware of what computers and software can do (and seeing a PowerPoint show at least once a day anyway), will be more impressed with visuals that are hand-crafted and show the mark of human touch. This can be anything from a Stephen Holl watercolor sketch to a pastel drawing to a cardboard study model. Next time you're planning visual aids for a presentation, consider whether the Inversion Principle might not apply to your current challenge. As always, remember that your objective should determine the means, not the other way around.

ural behavior. Along with this insecurity comes the fear of looking foolish, of making a wrong mark, or of not knowing what to draw at the moment of truth. All of these concerns are valid, but none are necessarily invincible. Knowing which marks to make in the presentation room is the difference between speaking *ex tempore* and improvisation. No one expects you to make things up as you go along. The extemporaneous speaker draws from a deep well of knowledge of the subject, and his or her illustrations flow naturally from having thought deeply about the topic well in advance of the presentation.

Summing It Up

Visual aids are an essential part of the presenter's toolbox—even more so if the presenter is a design professional. A presentation without visual aids often resembles a sermon—and a boring one at that.

Presenters are responsible for their own props; that responsibility can be delegated, but it cannot be avoided.

Presentation tools discussed in this chapter include:

- *Presentation boards.* Tried-and-true, but also expensive and cumbersome.
- *Slides.* Once a staple of the profession, now falling out of favor.
- *Traditional overheads.* Never much used by architects, an excellent tool for tabular or diagrammatic data.
- *Computer overheads.* Rapidly becoming pervasive, able to combine many different media in a single source.
- *Models.* Another time-honored tool; expensive and surprisingly abstract, but helpful for clients who can't read drawings.
- *Computer animation and video.* Also seeing a rapid increase in use, animations are powerful and impressive but communicate less than meets the eye.
- *Real-time graphics.* If you really want to dazzle the audience, do what you do best: draw for them.

Know When to Get Off

10

"Darling, for a speech to be immortal, it
need not be interminable."
——MURIEL HUMPHREY

"Never talk for more than twenty minutes."
——RONALD REAGAN

In the days before karaoke bars, you could sometimes find a tavern where patrons were permitted,
even encouraged, to entertain the audience. At one
such bar in New York City's theater district, performers from Broadway shows would take turns
with civilians. One sure way to tell the professionals
from the amateurs was that the professionals always
knew when they were done. The amateurs often had
to be told.

Knowing when to get off, having the sense to leave
before your audience has gotten tired of you, may be
the one of the least-developed skills among professionals who give formal presentations. Mercifully,
many presentations are time-limited, which means
that the audience can give you the hook if you over-

stay your welcome. But anyone who has presented more than a few times knows that a co-presenter who doesn't understand this fundamental principle can send a well-crafted presentation up in smoke.

Timing Is Everything

Why are most presenters often time-impaired in the moment of truth? There are several possible reasons:

- ▶ The emotional energy of a presentation (nervousness, excitement, etc.) makes presenters lose track of time. This is something of a cliché, but it happens to be true.

- ▶ When faced with a "do or die" situation—competing for a project, for instance—presenters tend to say more than they intended to say.

- ▶ No one actually bothered to find out how long it would take the boss to read his or her two-page, single-spaced introduction. Turns out it was more than double the allotted time.

- ▶ Although the individual components were carefully honed, no one bothered to account for the transitions from one speaker to another, or changes in media (from projection to boards, for example) during the presentation.

Just as there are many reasons for screwing up planned time allotments during a presentation, there are many possible treatments for the problem. Following are a few suggestions for making your presentations run more smoothly to an unhurried conclusion.

The Soul of Wit

The essence of knowing when to get off is not over-taxing the audience's patience. In a karaoke bar, that usually means one song to a customer. In a professional presentation, it means finishing within the allotted time—better still, finishing with time to spare. Marketing presentations are almost always structured with a certain interval for presenting, followed by a defined period for questions and answers. Thinking back to the discussions on interaction in Chapters 2 and 5, it should be apparent that more interaction—in the form of questions and answers—is preferable to more one-sided talking. Design presentations can be looser, but even so, an ending time is usually set for most design meetings. In civic presentations (zoning hearings and the like) brevity is even more essential, as commissioners and other officials tire very quickly of presentations they may not even be interested in.

If finishing on (or ahead of) schedule is the goal, why do presenters so seldom achieve it? Besides the answers given above, the primary reason is that, commonly, architects plan to fail in this area. Not that they *try* to fail, but that failure is the frequent result of trying to present too much information, being overly optimistic about how long it takes to cover a point, and not building in a time margin for the realities of the presentation itself. Let's take a look at some intentional strategies for knowing when to get off.

Loose Planning

Many presentations are doomed from the outset (with respect to time) because they are poorly planned. Someone volunteers to cover the firm's credentials in five minutes, then loads up two carousels of slides (or their computer equivalent) to take to the presentation. Loose planning means taking a realistic look at what you have to say, allocating sufficient time to the topic, and then actually reducing what needs to be covered to allow for plenty of improvisation.

Loose planning also means that you allow reasonable time for the points that need to be covered; it does not mean sloppy or careless planning. It's amazing how speakers seem unable to think in less than five-minute increments, as though a two- or three-minute thought or idea is inconceivable. Unless you have all day to make a presentation, your loose planning should account for every minute of time available. Planning for agenda items of less than a minute suggests that either you are a super-skilled presenter or you have an unrealistic idea of how long it takes a design professional to complete a thought.

Reality Margin

This brings up another key aspect of making timing work better in your presentations: Build margin into the schedule. If you have a very tight presentation window—say twenty or thirty minutes total, you will want to make every second count. But you still should allocate a minute between each major segment of your presentation for movement, media changing, a quick question, or just a chance for people to catch their breath. Paradoxically, the less time you have to present, the more critical it becomes to build margin into your schedule.

Tight Execution

The flip side of loose planning is tight execution. If you plan with plenty of margin, and execute precisely, the worst thing that can happen is that you finish your presentation early, which, from the point of view of your listeners, is a gift of great value.

Tight execution requires attention to detail. It means having as much of your show set up in advance of the meeting as possible. It means knowing the space you're presenting in, and not having to hunt for an electrical outlet. It means knowing who's responsible for the easels, who's responsible for the boards, and who's responsible for flipping the lights on and off. It means knowing each other's in-cues and out-cues (see the sidebar, "Managing Multiple Characters"). And it means having a "stage manager," a person designated to be responsible for sticking to the schedule, even if it means interrupting one of the presenters to tell him or her it's time to move on. Achieving tight execution is not difficult, but it is intentional. No one ever finishes a presentation on time by accident.

"Always leave the audience wanting more."
—Show business maxim

Setting the Pace

One aspect of managing the time well in a presentation is thinking about the pace. This relates to, but is not the same as, the discussion of energy in Chapter 5. The pace of a presentation can vary from one presenter to the next, but there is a contagious quality to pace. If one presenter begins with a slow, lethargic delivery, it is likely that the next person up to speak will follow suit, unless he or she is thinking about pace and the need to liven things up. Conversely, if the first presenter out of the chute is lively and ener-

RULE OF THUMB

As in a relay race, the first presenter will set the pace for your presentation (whether you like it or not).

gized, it is likely that other presenters will be more upbeat.

The obvious implication is that you should lead off a multiperson presentation not just with your most senior person or your "best" presenter, but with a person who will set the pace for the rest of the team. If a slow talker insists on going first, make doubly sure that a highly energized person, one who can reset the pace of the presentation to a more reasonable level, follows him or her immediately. Remember that the audience can listen a lot faster than you can talk, and few audiences ever complain about a presenter going too fast. When they do, it usually means the presenter was assuming too much with respect to professional jargon and construction terms, not that they were actually talking too fast.

Varying the Pace

> "The right word may be effective, but no word was ever as effective as a rightly timed pause."
> —MARK TWAIN

You've probably heard a band leader say, "I'd like to slow things down for a moment." Musicians, even rock musicians, recognize that you can't go full tilt all the time. While it may not be professional to say, "I'd like to slow things down," you need to recognize that a presentation, particularly a long one, really shouldn't go at the same pace from start to finish. If one of your presenters is particularly energetic, it might be wise to follow him or her with a person who's more, shall we say, relaxed in his or her delivery. If you are presenting solo, it becomes even more important to say (if only to yourself), "I'd like to slow it down for a moment." Your solo presentation is even more in need of variety in pace than the presentation involving multiple speakers.

On the other side of the coin, if you notice that a presentation is dragging, if each presenter seems more lethargic than the last, you may need to follow the advice of Chef Emeril Lagasse and "kick it up a notch." In extreme cases, you might actually have to interject a more animated speaker (or comment, at least) in an unexpected lull in your program. Going off your agenda, in this instance, is probably less of a sin than allowing a dull presentation to grow even duller.

In any event, listen to the pace of your next presentation, whether alone or in concert with others, and make a mental note of whether it might be wise to "slow things down a bit" or to "kick it up a notch" instead.

Orchestrating Movement

Another area that is critical to finishing on time is managing the movement of a presentation. In the theater, this planned movement is called "blocking," and it may surprise you to learn that plays as well as movies and television programs are blocked to an amazing level of specificity—particularly the latter two, where lighting and focus are dependent on actors hitting their marks correctly. Yet architects somehow feel that if they have four or six or ten presenters in a room, somehow they will all figure out when to stand and when to sit, where to walk and where not to, by some mystical inner knowledge. The fact is that an unblocked presentation with more than one presenter is a major source of embarrassment, confusion, and wasted time.

You might argue, "But I thought spontaneous movement was supposed to be a good thing." When you have the stage to yourself, it is a good thing. Blocking is most important when more than one person is speaking to the same point, when you are transitioning from one speaker to another, or when there are important changes to the setting that must be made by the presenters because you left your stage crew back at the office.

Blocking is not difficult; it is simply a set of instructions for what each presenter should be doing at each moment of the presentation. It can be as specific as, "At the moment Bill dims the lights, Jack rises and moves to Jill's left, at which point Jill hands Jack the remote." Blocking doesn't need to be written out, as long as *each presenter has his or her own blocking written down* on his or her "script," a presentation outline, or copy of the agenda. And, of course, by the time of the actual presentation, everyone should be "off book," stage jargon for knowing their lines *and their blocking* by heart.

Striking the Set

Getting off the stage can be an awkward moment if you haven't thought about it beforehand. "Striking the set" is stage jargon for disassembling a production when it is over. The key idea in striking the set is to get your stuff out of the room as quickly and as unobtrusively as possible. This doesn't mean that you may not shake hands with various members of the audience or exchange small pleasantries, but it's best to do those things while your team is packing, not to assume that your equipment will vanish on its own.

Managing Multiple Characters

It's amazing that almost no one thinks about the physical management of the different persons and personalities in a presentation. The solo presentation is a relatively rare thing—often, you are one of a team of presenters that may be as small as two or as large as a dozen. Obviously, the importance of blocking your presentation increases proportionately with the number of presenters.

The most important task is for someone to assume the role of director—to take on the task of telling people where to stand. The director's job in this instance is to manage the characters, giving everyone a supportive role, whether they are speaking or not, and making sure that all the technical issues are covered. When a person is not talking, they should be seated quietly, with their full attention focused on the person who is presenting, or they can be managing lights, opening and closing blinds, punching the Page Down key on the laptop, or taking copious notes of everything that is being said. It's the director's job to make sure that there is no wasted motion, no redundant activity, and no confusion about who needs to be where, when. Sometimes in a presentation, the director also needs to be the prompter, either reminding people that they are "on deck," and should be moving into place, or politely informing a time-challenged speaker that it's time to move on.

Multicharacter presentations often fail in the handoffs from one speaker to another. Presenters seem to follow the model of a ritualized panel discussion, where each speaker is introduced with great solemnity, and then proceeds to restate his or her own introduction as though the introduction had never been made; there are also many "thank you" exchanges. The whole process has the ritualized aspect of Kabuki theater. Besides wasting time, these transitions are tedious and unnecessary.

For a better way to manage transitions from one speaker to another, watch your local television news. Newscasters use two techniques to manage the handoff. In one, they simply start talking when their partner is finished, with no acknowledgment of the counterpart at all. This method works amazingly well in technical presentations, saves valuable time, and has the added benefit of making you look like you know what you're doing.

The second technique newscasters use to arrange a handoff, usually to the weatherperson or the sportscaster, is to ask a question that only he or she would have the answer to. "What do you think, Bob? Is it going to rain on the St. Patrick's Day parade tomorrow?" Bob, chuckling, answers the question as a lead-in to his forecast. This lighthearted banter (which becomes annoying if overdone) is actually a smooth way to move from one speaker to another without the over-elaborate ritual handoff that is common in design presentations. So instead of saying, "Now our project manager, Jill Stevens, is going to tell you how we plan to manage the project," you could try, "Jill, there's a lot to do in the next twelve months. How are we going to get it all done?" The effect is less formal, less stiff, and reinforces the collegial nature of the profession.

First, you need an exit line. Your exit line needs to be something stronger than, "Well, I guess that's it." It should be a clarion call to the action you wish your audience to take (hire your firm, approve the design), and it should make it abundantly clear that your presentation is over. "Thank you very much" is universally understood to be such a line, but it suffers from overuse and lack of specificity. You should

Help for the Timing-impaired

On nearly every presentation team there is often one person who, besides being a competent professional and a pleasure to work with, has no sense of time in a presentation setting. Reasons for this impairment were discussed at the beginning of this chapter. In most cases, it seems incurable, although the more presentations one does, the more likely he or she is to overcome this impairment. On the other hand, if your role is to manage a presentation, to see to it that all the presenters get their fair share of "air time," you may need to provide some preventive care to ensure that a person with no sense of time doesn't ruin the flow of the presentation.

What to do?

▶ Make sure the time-insensitive person knows exactly what's expected. If he or she has five minutes to talk, encourage the speaker to plan for something more like four minutes, explaining that we all tend to get a little wordy when the pressure is on.

▶ Suggest that the person script his or her remarks, pointing out that a single page of normal typing, single-spaced, can take five minutes to read.

▶ Work closely with the person to make certain that his or her remarks can fit within your timeframe. This may require more rehearsal than is customary or comfortable, but it becomes a necessity when dealing with a person who tends to ramble. The more the person goes over his or her spiel, the less likely it is to mutate in the presentation room.

▶ Threaten the hook, if you have to. Work out a system of signals to give your wayward presenter if he or she is veering off the topic or threatening to go over the time allotment (though not surprisingly, the time-impaired are also usually impervious to hand signals). Let the presenter know in advance that any breach of the programmed time will result in a likely interruption. No one wants to get the hook.

give some thought to what your last line will be. After you give your exit line, don't immediately walk off the stage. Make eye contact with your audience for a moment, to let them know that you've done your best. Then you (and other members of your team) should stand, and move briskly to tear down your presentation setup. This can be an awkward time if you haven't planned for the logistics of withdrawal as well as the logistics of entry. Like every other part of your presentation, roles should be assigned. A very small team can strike an elaborate presentation in a very few minutes if it has been planned ahead.

Summing It Up

Timing is everything, particularly in time-sensitive presentations. Overstaying your welcome is a cardinal sin in presenting as in show business. Recognizing that a well-delivered presentation requires more than just casual attention to the demands of timing is half the battle. Here are some reminders to help you and your team know when to get off:

- ► *Loose planning.* Plan to say less than would be necessary to fill the available time.

- ► *Reality margin.* Recognize in your planning that people will say more than they intended and that changeovers do not happen instantly, and leave margin for interaction.

- ► *Tight execution.* Once you are in the room, work to stay on your planned schedule. Other than spontaneous interaction with the audience—a good problem—discipline your team to stay on course, even if it means interrupting someone who goes off.

- *Set the pace.* Make sure your leadoff presenter is someone who can set a lively, energetic pace for the rest of the team to follow.
- *Managing multiple characters.* The director (you) needs to let everyone know where to sit, when to stand, and what to bring into the room. It may seem demeaning, but it's much less demeaning than looking like the Keystone Kops because your team of professionals doesn't know what to do.
- *Help for the time-impaired.* Make sure notoriously windy speakers know exactly what's expected, and work closely with them to hone their remarks to fit your timeframe. Let them know that you will interrupt if they wander too far afield.

Epilog: Five Minutes!

"Everyone has butterflies in their stomach. The difference between the pros and the amateurs is that the pros get theirs to fly in formation."

— ZIG ZIGLAR

Perhaps you've seen one of the dozens of show-biz movies made in the twentieth century where the new/aging/lovestruck/depressed star is putting on her makeup in one of those lighted mirrors that betoken "professional show business." Suddenly, there's an anonymous knock at the door. "Five minutes!" calls the disembodied voice on the other side. The star jumps in her chair. It's time to go on! Will she be ready? Will you?

This chapter can be thought of as a last-minute checklist of critical items to review as you prepare to enter the arena. Running down this list will help you gain confidence if you have given reasonable attention to all the items on it. With five minutes to go, here's what you need to be ready to go on.

Physical Preparation

Discussed at length in Chapter 1, the importance of physical preparation cannot be overstated. Presenting is a physical activity as much as it is a mental one, and being physically underprepared is a leading cause of stage fright. Some quick ideas for being physically ready to present:

- ▶ Get a good night's sleep the night before the presentation. Carousing the night before will not make you a better presenter.

- ▶ If at all possible, get some exercise the day of your presentation. It will help you be alert and "in the moment."

- ▶ Combat tension at the moment of truth by using tension/relaxation drills, isometric exercises that use tension creatively to break tension.

- ▶ Take note of, and command of, the space that is available to you as a presenter.

- ▶ Remember that presenting is a dance. Even if you are neither athletic nor graceful, the audience wants to see how you move in connection with your presentation.

Motivation Review

The second commandment of show business, discussed in Chapter 2, is "What's My Motivation?" More than any technical point, your objective for the presentation needs to be the foremost thing in your mind as you talk. Your motivation informs the inflection of every word you say. Think about the specific action you would like your audience to take as a result of hearing you speak, and make the realization of that action your motivating force.

In a marketing presentation, your motivation is probably "to get the job." That may or may not be a realistic objective, based on a number of factors that are, at the moment you present, outside your control. Unless this is a project you really oughtn't lose, a better motivation might be to clearly communicate your firm's qualifications in such a compelling way that the client will consider you for *a* project, if not the one in view at the moment.

TIP

Think about the specific action you would like your audience to take as a result of hearing you speak, and make the realization of that action your motivating force.

In design presentations, most likely your goal is to gain approval for your work. Again, that motivation is straightforward but may miss the mark slightly as well. Depending on how closely you have worked with the client, consider whether a better goal might be to explain your work in such a clear way that there can be no doubt of its alignment with your client's goals. While this distinction may seem subtle, it takes the pressure off you to "sell" your idea to the "customer," who may not in fact want what it is you're asking him or her to buy.

In requests before a review agency, such as a planning or zoning commission, your motivation will likely be, simply, to move the project forward, not to have it continued to the next meeting or be told, as Dorothy was by the Wizard of Oz, that there are new requirements for you to meet. This motivation, to keep the project moving ahead, is probably a good animating force for a hearing. You should remember that the commissioners might care a good deal less about the architecture than you do. They may also care a good deal more about how the dumpsters are screened from neighboring landowners than you do, as well.

While in-house, professional, and other presentations are less at the core of professional practice, having a clear motivation is even more important to keep them from becoming a tedious, informative presentation that could be delivered better by a Web site. Think carefully about a specific action that you want your audience to take after they hear your talk, and then go for it with all you've got!

Mental Confidence

Near the top of presenters' worst fears is "not remembering what I'm supposed to say," or similar sentiments expressed in different words. Being tongue-tied is often a result of poor physical preparation, as discussed above. As often or more often, it's the result of knowing less about the subject than you should. Because most design professionals are certified as competent by the state, they mistakenly assume that what they need to know for a presentation will be readily available to them when the time comes. Sadly, many learn that professional competence does not always equal presenting competence or confidence.

Confidence comes from, not surprisingly, being a master of your topic. This means knowing more, much more, about the subject than you will ever have to say. When you have a surplus of knowledge of a topic, it is easy to speak confidently, casually, and extemporaneously, drawing from the surplus rather than sucking up the last few droplets of information from a nearly dry well. It would be nice if some rhetorical device could substitute for mastery of the topic, but regrettably, none has been found.

"Knowing your lines" for a presenter doesn't mean having memorized a script. It means knowing

Don't Take Yourself So Seriously

If you are physically warmed up and fully in command of your subject, is it still possible to get "locked up" in a presentation? Experience should tell you that it is. Even capable presenters who take pains to be physically ready to present are sometimes overcome with nerves. The final remaining cause of stage fright, when you have prepared both physically and mentally to give a good talk, is taking yourself—and your task—too seriously.

This is, like the other causes of stage fright, surprisingly common in the design professions. Architects and designers tend to view presentations as life-or-death situations on which their entire future depends. Needless to say, this attitude lends itself more to nerves and stiffness than to fluidity and grace in presenting.

But many presentations that professionals give *are* important—some extremely so. A presentation may be the difference between continued prosperity and downsizing staff, or between a project moving ahead and being stalled by a review committee. How can you not take yourself seriously when the stakes are so high?

The answer is not to minimize the importance of the task, but to keep yourself relaxed. Apart from the absolutely essential physical preparation already mentioned, and having command of your subject, here are some tips to keep the pressure at bay when you feel as though everything is riding on a presentation:

> ► *Get some perspective*. Seriously. Drive by a busy playground, or a homeless shelter, or a retirement home on your way to the presentation. Consider how what you are presenting affects the elderly, or the very young, or people with no regular means of support. Chances are good that it doesn't affect these people much, or at all. Put your monumental challenge in context with what's going on in the rest of the world, and it won't look so huge and intimidating.

> ► *Get off your high horse*. This presentation doesn't depend entirely on you. It never does. Unless you are a sole practitioner without even an office assistant, there are other capable people involved, people whose goal is to make you look good. Give them some credit for being able to do just that.

> ► *Assume the best*. View your audience as a group that wants to be entertained; to learn about you, your firm, or your project; to see you do well. There are actually very few sadists in the real estate and construction industry, although every architect claims to know most of them personally. The fact is that most of the people you will present to—the vast majority—want you to do well, to have a great presentation, and to enjoy their time with you. The actual number of people wishing you to fail is infinitesimally small by comparison.

> ► *Do kid yourself*. One pair of professional colleagues used to loosen up before each presentation by reminding themselves of "The Three Cs": "We're confident, we're competent, and we're continent." This never failed to take the edge off an otherwise tense moment waiting for a presentation to start. Humor directed at yourself is just as effective at defusing tension as it is with the group you're speaking to. If you're humor-impaired, have someone tell you a joke just before you present.

a topic inside and out to the extent that a script is unnecessary; that no question can throw you off your game; and that you could, if needed, discourse for ten times longer than the time allotted for the presentation. The real genius comes in knowing which 10 percent to say, and which 90 percent to save for another time.

Know the Room

In Chapter 4, "Find Your Light," a number of considerations of the physical environment are raised. None, however, is as important or basic as familiarity with the space. No self-respecting performers would stride onto an unknown stage in full costume, regardless of how well they know their routine. Other elements of "finding your light" include:

- ➤ Understanding the space you have for your presentation, including walls, windows, chairs, risers, or whatever else may or may not be present.

- ➤ Setting the stage: putting movable furnishings in a position that will best suit the objectives of your presentation.

- ➤ Planning for all necessary contingencies (extension cords!) and even a few less obvious things (like what you'll do if your projector blows a fuse).

- ➤ Performing a "sound check" to know how you'll work with microphones, if required by the presentation format, or if not, how your voice will carry in the space.

- ➤ Don't forget the light itself, even if the architect who designed the room you're presenting in did. If the audience can't see you, they can't hear you, either. Presenting is not radio—it's television.

▶ If you absolutely, positively can't gain access to a space in advance of your presentation, you need to be even more prepared for any and every eventuality. This means more redundancy, more preparation, and more risk for you and your team.

Face Out

Presenting is more like ballet than modern dance. It is important to keep your smiling face oriented toward the audience for almost every instant you are presenting, the way a spinning ballerina turns her head far faster than her body to keep facing out at all times. Obviously, this can't happen if you're absorbed in talking to your presentation boards.

More than just literally facing out, "facing out" has to do with five key attitudes that can make the difference between lively, memorable presentations and the merely competent ones:

REMINDER

Remember the Five E's of Facing Out: Energy, Empathy, Engagement, Enthusiasm, and Entertainment.

▶ *Energy.* Your pitch (frequency) plus your pace (in words per minute) equals your energy. Animation helps, but it won't help much if you're talking so slowly that the audience is nodding off.

▶ *Empathy.* The line of connection between you and your audience. Empathy is created through the recognition of common background, common experience, common modes of dress or communication, shared values, and self-deprecating humor to show you're not a stuffed shirt.

▶ *Engagement.* Engage your audience in a discussion; it's far more interesting to them than a lecture, and it increases the likelihood that you'll reach your objective for the presentation. The easiest way to engage: ask questions, and be willing to wait for an answer.

➤ *Enthusiasm*. The hardest of the "five E's" to fake, enthusiasm is the actual attitude you bring to a presentation, separate from the content. If you are not excited to be making the presentation, your audience will know it within seconds. Enthusiasm requires internal motivation; it can't be gotten from another person, although there is a contagious element in it.

➤ *Entertainment*. No presentation should be entirely without entertainment. Most often, that means appropriate humor, although it may involve your vacation slides if you're humor-impaired. Entertainment is not purposeless: it relieves tension, builds empathy, and humanizes both the presenter and the audience.

Overcoming Obstacles

RULE OF THUMB

Professionals have the poise and experience to take unexpected glitches in their presentations in stride.

The biggest obstacle to overcome in a presentation is the mistaken belief that there won't be any obstacles. Every production, from the community playhouse to the Metropolitan Opera, is beset with glitches, flubs, and screwups large and small. What separates the amateurs from the professionals is how they react to these problems. Professionals have the poise and experience to take them in stride.

Preventable obstacles should be anticipated before the presentation itself, and reasonable measures taken to ensure that either they won't happen or, if they do, that you have another method readily at hand to accomplish your goal.

Unpreventable obstacles are usually the ones brought into the room by members of the audience, not by you or by the setting itself. Often, these obstacles involve hostility on the part of one or more audience members. Remember the AARP method of handling inappropriate feedback:

- ▶ *Acknowledge.* Recognize the person and the fact that he or she has made a statement, even an inappropriate one.

- ▶ *Affirm.* Let the speaker know that you clearly understood what he or she said, without necessarily agreeing with it.

- ▶ *Record.* Make an obvious point of writing down, preferably in a visible, public way, the essence of the speaker's comment.

- ▶ *Persevere.* Get on with your presentation without judging whether the inappropriate feedback was relevant or not.

No Need to Raise Your Voice

Projection is the art of filling the room with your voice without shouting. The keys to projection are fairly simple:

- ▶ Size up the space in your sound check, to have an idea how loud you'll need to be.

- ▶ Support your voice with good posture and diaphragmatic breathing.

- ▶ Target the last person in the last row as the person who needs to hear you the most.

- ▶ If you are required to use a microphone, use it as a tool, not a substitute, for the practices described above.

Get Centered

While transcendental meditation is not required, you do need some conscious effort to stay "in the moment" while you present. Being in the moment allows you to acknowledge problems in your presentation without becoming derailed by them. At the simplest level, being in the moment embodies two very basic ideas: don't anticipate and don't reflect.

Don't Anticipate

Try to stay focused on what is being said, either by you or by someone else, whether that person is a member of your team or of the audience. React in real time to questions and problems, rather than letting your mind move ahead of the immediate present. What you need to say five minutes from now will be there when it needs to be. What you need to be thinking about right now is right now.

Don't Reflect

In the same way, you need to let the past slip away in a presentation. If you dwell on mistakes, missed cues, things that didn't go as well as you would have liked, you will reap the negative dividends of those mishaps over and over again. No presentation ever goes perfectly, even a Broadway show (*especially* a Broadway show!). The thing that separates the amateurs from the pros is the latters' ability to overcome glitches, fix them to the extent that they're repairable, and stay in the moment.

Think about Visual Aids

Every architect uses visuals in presentations—it is the rare design professional who doesn't. The key is to think about which visual media will be most likely to achieve your objective for the presentation, and prepare your exhibits accordingly. Most architects do the same thing time after time because they are comfortable with a format or because they know what's involved in its preparation. These are two of the weakest possible reasons to choose a visual aid medium. Some of the many options available to presenters include:

- ► *Slide projection*. An old standby that usually requires a darkened room, which can lead at times to audience disengagement.

- ► *Presentation boards*. Another old reliable, boards are the technology least likely to break in the presentation room—assuming you can get them to the presentation room. They can also be expensive and somewhat cumbersome depending on how many you need.

- ► *Traditional overhead projection (foils)*. A medium little used by architects because of its low fidelity to photographs, it's actually an excellent way to present tabular or simple graphic information.

- ► *Computerized overhead projection*. Taking the profession by storm is the use of presentation software, used with a laptop computer and an LCD projector. Presenters need to be comfortable with this technology, and have a backup in case the equipment fails, as happens more than occasionally.

- ► *Models*. What better way to describe three-dimensional spaces than in three dimensions? Models sometimes suffer because clients can't understand their scale, but people do love to look at (and play with) them.

Epilog: Five Minutes!

► *Computer animations and fly-throughs.* Though the profession still struggles to put together a convincing "virtual reality" exhibit of a project, animations and fly-throughs are improving every year. Consider, however, the passivity of watching a programmed animation versus interacting with the design in some other way.

REMINDER
Time management begins with realistic expectations about what can be said in the allotted time, generous budgeting for questions, and tight execution of personnel and scenery changes.

Plan Your Exit

Most presenters "run long" from the sheer excitement of presenting. Good presenters plan for this and budget time generously, recognizing that virtually every participant in a presentation will say more than he or she intended. Time management begins with having realistic expectations about what can be said in the allotted time, budgeting generously for overtalking, and executing tightly in terms of personnel and scenery changes.

Many presenters are tripped up by such rudimentary problems as not allowing themselves time to set up or tear down their exhibits, not planning for transitions between speakers, and not disciplining the team to stay within their allotted time. Even if it seems rude, both your team and your audience will appreciate your reining in a rambler who's left the reservation. The alternative is to punish the important part of your presentation so that the least-capable presenter can have more time.

And don't forget to plan how you're going to get off the stage. Some of the most awkward moments in presenting come from design professionals who have finished speaking but have no way of signaling to the audience that they are. Best plan: Have a compelling exit line that begs for applause, or at least acknowledges that you're done talking!

Last-minute Checks

Few things are as nerve-wracking as the final few minutes leading up to a big presentation. Breathing becomes shallow and perspiration uncontrollable, and previously clear points become muddled in the final few moments before you go on. Rather than sitting and thinking about how nervous you are, put the last seconds before you go onstage to productive use. (We'll assume that you've done all the proper preparation already.)

- ► *Conduct a physical inventory.* Check for tension, shallow breathing, nervous habits, and manage each appropriately. Using the restroom might be wise at this point.

- ► *Review the basics.* What is your motivation? What are the principal points that support your objective? Are they clear in your mind and the minds of your colleagues?

- ► *Preset.* Is there any part of your presentation that can be set up ahead of time (easels, for example) that will save you time when you move into the presentation room? (But be careful not to overdo this—don't, for example, boot up your laptop if you will only have to shut it down and reboot it once you're in the room.)

- ► *Review.* Run down the order of the presentation with your team one last time. It's never too late to catch a misunderstanding.

- ► *Focus.* Turn off your cell phone or pager, put away that other project file you're working on, and get focused on the task at hand.

- ► *Relax.* Tell yourself a joke, or get someone else to, to take your mind off the earth-shattering importance of what you're about to do.

> *Relax some more.* Remind yourself that you know what you're doing, you're as prepared as it's humanly possible to be, and your audience is prepared to like you.

Curtain Up!

Even if you follow every word of advice that you have read in this book, that moment when the gate-keeper for the selection committee or the chair of the zoning board says, "You may begin," is still like diving off a cliff into an ice-cold mountain stream. The only preparation for that moment is to have faced it before. The more times you dive from that cliff, the less shocking the water is when you hit it. Half the battle is recognizing how that moment galvanizes your entire body, turning you into either a lean, mean presenting machine or a mass of quivering protoplasm. Unfortunately, your specific response to the moment of truth cannot be rehearsed, no matter how much time you devote to practicing your talk. You may even find that each time you present, some new part of your body (your knees, your stomach, your chest) reacts in a totally new and unexpected way.

This is the excitement of live theater. It is always new, never the same twice, and often just as thrilling for the performer as it is for the audience. This is the dance that the audience has come to see—how will you perform when the spotlight is on you and you alone? It is indeed a "moment of truth," because no matter how skilled you are, no matter how many times you've presented in the past, there will be a new surprise for you each time the curtain goes up. If it ever stops being a surprise, it's time to find a new career.

Ultimately, it is this exhilarating moment when you are onstage that makes presenting one of the performing arts, and distinguishes it from most of the rest of the practice of a design profession. In your office, you can control almost everything, and those things you can't control can be managed over time. When you are giving a presentation, you are reacting in real time to a group whose reactions you can only guess at, whose responses are unpredictable, and whose interests may or may not be the same as yours. If the imagery is suggestive of a thrill ride, it's because that's exactly what presenting is. Either you embrace the dynamic, untamed quality of it or you will be continually frustrated in your efforts to make your presentation into a controlled intellectual download—something it was never meant to be.

So as a final suggestion, and a philosophy from which to view the art of presenting, draw a line down the center of a piece of paper. On the left side of the line, write every word that describes presentations that neither you nor anyone else would want to watch: boring, informative, stiff, lifeless, dull, monotonous, and so on. On the right side of the line, write words that describe how you would like your presentations to be perceived: dynamic, engaging, enthusiastic, motivating, energizing. Now look at your two lists. Which list is suggestive of talking? Which list is suggestive of dancing? Now go and dance.

Appendix: Using Presentation Software

Because computer-driven presentations have become such a staple of professional presentations, presenters need some basic guidelines for using the software that drives the presentation. The most common presentation software is Microsoft's PowerPoint, but other products with similar features perform the same function: they enable you to compose a virtual "slide show" on your computer, which can be projected by an LCD projector to an audience of virtually any size. These programs are feature-rich, and it is not within the scope of this appendix to provide a complete user manual. Rather, you will learn some useful techniques and functions that can help your presentations sing. More important, you will learn some features and functions to avoid.

The Basics

Once you have made an informed decision to go ahead with a computer-based presentation, you need to quickly "storyboard" the key sections of the presentation. You can make a list of major themes on a piece of paper, or you can use the presentation software's "outline" mode to work directly on the computer. There are two advantages to the latter approach: You can change your mind and move pieces of the outline around very easily; and, when your storyboard is done, you've already begun the work of entering the headlines into your presentation file. As with any computer-based task, you should save your work early and often.

As your presentation develops, you can easily add "slides" under the major headings. You can also rearrange your presentation on a virtual "light box," a view that shows all (or most) of your presentation's slides at once. If you're thinking about deleting a slide but are not entirely sure you want to, don't hit the Delete key; choose instead to "hide" the slide— it'll stay in the file, but won't show up in the presentation unless you choose to "unhide" it later.

Words: Less Is More

Because entering text into presentation software is so easy, it's also easy to overdo. You can even import outlines (or entire paragraphs) from your word-processing program if you want. But this capability points up one of the greatest hazards of presentation software: the tendency to put too much information on the screen. In the first place, presentation slides that are too wordy are difficult for the audience to read. More significantly, they tempt you to read the slide to your audience, which is the biggest no-no in using presentation software. Nothing insults and annoys an audience more than a presenter staring at a screen that reads, "Over 25 years' experience in the design of elementary, secondary, and higher-ed facilities," and then saying aloud, "Over 25 years' experience in the design of elementary, secondary, and higher-ed facilities." Which leads to presentation software commandment number one.

Use Headlines, Not Sentences

An appropriate headline for the factoid in the previous paragraph might be, "Abundant Education Experience" (see Figure A.1). Those three words would be sufficient to cue you to say the statement about your firm's elementary, secondary, and higher-ed experience, without giving away the point to the audience beforehand. If you have ever seen a presenter read bullet points to the audience, you

TIP

Bullet points should be headlines, not complete sentences or paragraphs.

Our firm has been in business for 24 years

- We have serviced numerous public, private and parochial school clients while maintaining a high quality of design.
- Our client service reputation is second to none.

Wrong way: the wordy approach

24 years' experience:

- School clients:
  - -public
  - -private
- Service reputation

Right way: bullets and headlines

Figure A.1

know how tiresome this can become after just one or two screensful of text. An hour-long presentation delivered in this manner can be deadly.

Pictures: Less Is Also More

Because architects and designers tend to be visually oriented, professionals love to load their computer-driven presentations with images. By and large, this is a good thing, and makes one wish that other business professionals would use more pictures. But because designers normally deal with large, high-quality images, there is a tendency to assume that presentations should include large, high-quality image files in order to present the work to best advantage. Surprisingly, this is simply not the case.

First a principle, then some arithmetic. The principle is that images projected on a screen—any screen, including a CRT (cathode-ray tube), a monitor, or a projection screen—don't need to be nearly as information-rich as images printed on a page. The viewer's mind has a much easier time combining individual dots of information while looking at images on a screen. This is why computer monitors typically operate at around 75 dots per inch, while good printers (black-and-white or color) need at least 400 to 600 dots per inch—six to eight times as much information!—to create an acceptable level of quality. Knowing this principle will save you tremendous grief in preparing your computer presentations.

Now for some arithmetic. The single most important fact you need to know to put the right-size images in your presentation file is the resolution of your *projector*—not your laptop. The projected resolution—what goes on the screen—is in fact the *only*

TIP

The determining factor of image size in a computer presentation is the resolution of the projector, not the computer's screen.

relevant statistic. As stated previously, projectors continue to get better and cheaper with each passing year. Currently, projectors with 1,024 by 768 pixel resolution are common; soon they will be twice that good. The arithmetic principle is this: Any image that is larger than the maximum resolution of your projector contains wasted information. Wasted information has two major drawbacks: It slows down your presentation by making your computer work harder than is necessary, and it makes your presentation files unduly large, which wastes storage space, especially if, like most people, you are loathe to discard a presentation after it has been presented.

Further complicating this issue is the fact that most presenters like to leave a little margin around images in presentations, so that the graphic theme of the presentation is maintained from slide to slide. So if your projector has a maximum horizontal resolution of 1,024 pixels, and if you plan to have any margin at all on your graphics, it could reasonably be asserted that no image in the presentation need be more than 1,000 pixels wide. It bears pointing out that some photo-editing software, and most publishing software, deals with pixels per inch, or ppi. This particular measurement is irrelevant in the context of presenting. The only number that matters is the *total number of pixels in the image*, and width is usually the limiting dimension. So look at each image you place in a presentation file to ensure that it is no larger than the maximum resolution of the projector you plan to use. With the space-saving JPEG (Joint Photographic Experts Group) or GIF (Graphics Interchange Format) formats, you'll be amazed how little space the graphics will require in a fairly elaborate presentation file.

How do you get from large image files to small image files? Regrettably, this is a function that most presentation software cannot perform. If you shrink the image in the presentation program by adjusting its size, you will have made the picture smaller on the screen; you will not have reduced the size of the embedded image file. To make your high-resolution marketing images or renderings the right size for presenting, you will need to use photo-editing software (Adobe Photoshop or one of its numerous competitors) to actually *change the pixel dimensions of the image file.* Just make sure that you are working on a *copy* of the high-resolution image, not the original scan, or your marketing staff will want your head on

Projected Plans

One of the most agonizing activities in the design profession is getting plan and elevation drawings from AutoCAD, the de facto standard program for architectural computer-aided drawing (CAD), into computer-driven presentation software. Despite the fact that both AutoCAD and most presentation programs can read and write numerous graphic file formats, the results of saving CAD drawings in another format, bitmap (.BMP) for example, and importing that file into a presentation are often horrendous. The more detail in the CAD drawing, it seems, the worse it appears in the presentation.

One solution, albeit an imperfect one, seems to be the Clipboard. This Windows or Macintosh subroutine, accessed by using the Copy or Cut commands on the Edit menu on most programs, copies information into memory for use in other documents or programs. Strangely, the Copy and Paste commands at present seem to be the best way to get CAD information into a computer-driven presentation. This requires you to select the objects you want to copy in AutoCAD, copy them to the Clipboard, then switch to your presentation program and paste the information into the appropriate slide. While much less convenient than saving CAD files as separate graphics files, it appears to have a higher probability of success—if success is defined as a CAD image that is readable in the presentation.

a platter the next time they try to print the image on paper!

Special Effects: Less Is Crucial

One of the biggest pitfalls in using presentation software is the large number of special effects available to the presenter. Because these programs tend to offer numerous such effects, users tend to want to experiment with many different ones in a presentation. This is a deadly sin, comparable to the mania surrounding fonts in the early days of desktop publishing. In the same way that having a hundred fonts is no excuse to use them all in a document, having dozens of special effects in a program is no reason to use them all in a presentation.

TIP
Use special effects (dissolves, fades, wipes, and builds) sparingly, if at all.

The argument for special effects is, in essence, "They will make my presentation less boring." Not only is this not true, it ignores an important fact: *You* are what will make your presentation less boring, not your presentation software. No one is amazed (anymore) at text that flies onto the screen. What will amaze your audience is your ability to step confidently through a presentation with minimal reliance on prompts from the screen (by knowing your lines).

There are several categories of special effects, each of which will be discussed briefly.

Slide Transitions

One useful effect is the transition from one slide to another. Using it will give your presentation greater continuity than if the image simply changes from one virtual slide to the next. Try several transitions, and choose one that seems unobtrusive and graceful to you. Apply the transition universally to all the slides in your show, and remember that slides you add at the last minute will not have the transition you chose unless you specify it. Obviously, avoid spectacular transitions (like spinning the contents of the screen) at all costs.

Builds

A build makes the bullet points or other features of a slide apparent one at a time. In the days of actual slides, it took four unique slides to create a four-point build. Now, you just have to specify which slide(s) to apply a build to.

Builds can be useful for, well, building a case slowly and methodically. By using a build to bring up your main points one at a time, rather than all at once, you can keep the audience from getting ahead of you. The only time that builds don't work well is when you are forced to move through a presentation at a rapid pace—in such cases, the time required to bring up the points individually will annoy both you and your audience.

As is the case with transitions, choose a build that seems tasteful and unobtrusive. The least obtrusive build is the one where the bullet points just appear one at a time without any effect at all. The decision whether or not to dim previous points as new ones appear (reducing their contrast so that they become less noticeable) is a matter of taste. It depends on whether the points are parts of a larger idea or individual ideas that stand on their own merit.

One often-overlooked feature of builds is that they can apply to graphic as well as to text information in a presentation. This means that you could show a rendering, for example, and then have a series of arrows, or circles, or callouts appear on it in a sequence that followed your plan for explaining the image to the audience. This feature is one of the most useful, and least used, of all the effects available in presentation software.

Sound Effects

Presentation software comes loaded with sound effects that can accompany the appearance of text or graphics on the screen. These effects range from squealing tires to clicking camera shutters and typewriter keys. Your decision to use sound effects should be a fairly simple one: Don't. The only exception to this rule is if you intend to make a humorous point, and the sound effect can serve as a punch line. Sound effects have been clinically shown to become annoying faster than any other special presentation effect.

TIP

The safest guide to using sound effects in a presentation is to not use them at all.

Templates

Presentation software is also loaded (or larded) with dozens, sometimes hundreds, of presentation templates, which allow neophyte presenters to create "professional-looking" presentations with a minimum of skill. As a design professional, you will find that these templates run the gamut from barely passable to truly awful. It is likely that you will use none of them in creating a presentation. It is more likely that you, or someone in your firm, will attempt to create a standard presentation template, which can be saved in a common file location, to serve as the basis for your firm's future presentations. It is likelier still that each presentation you make will come with an excuse to develop a new format or a new template. Don't worry about too much wasted effort. As a design professional, you have an obligation to rise above the commonplace in your presentation designs as much as in your work itself.

Autopilot

Another feature of presentation software is the capability to time your presentation in advance, changing the slides or bringing up bullet points at intervals you specify, either by entering the timing in a dialog box or by "recording" the timing as you punch through a presentation. While this tool might seem valuable for keeping you on track, it's actually very dangerous. As we discussed in Chapter 10, "Know When to Get Off," the timing of a live presentation very seldom matches the timing of a rehearsal or a run-through. People come up with new thoughts or new ways of expressing old thoughts that virtually guarantee your preset timing will be wrong. This could have the result of making you look like Lucy in the candy factory, frantically spitting out facts to keep up with your seemingly runaway presentation.

An even worse aspect of automatic timing, if one is needed, is that it makes your presentation seem automated. An audience that perceives you to be following a carefully scripted outline to keep in step with your automated presentation software will accord you the same credibility as a pitchman selling vegetable slicers at a county fair.

Adding Interactivity

As was hinted in Chapter 9, it is possible to make computer-driven presentations less linear than a traditional slide show, although 98 percent of presenters never bother to do it. Interactivity is a tremendous benefit of computer presenting, yet it is one that is seldom tried. It allows you to move to virtually any point in a presentation at the click of a mouse.

Appendix: Using Presentation Software

The way interactivity works is similar to building a simple web page, only much easier. You don't need to learn computer programming or a special language. Most presentation software allows you to insert a *hyperlink* onto a slide. A hyperlink is a word or phrase that functions as a button. When you click on that word or phrase during the "slide show" (the presentation mode of your presentation software), you immediately jump to a designated place in the show. It's a high-tech version of the children's game "Chutes and Ladders"; you are on a basically linear path, but have provided certain shortcuts that can move you forward or backward along that path in great leaps.

For example, if your presentation is structured around the four basic ideas of "experience," "personnel," "approach," and "management," you could insert a hyperlink on your first slide that would allow you to jump to any one of those sections of your presentation. You could then insert a "contents" link on each of the other slides that would take you back to the overview of the presentation. Or you could add three links to each slide, to allow you to jump instantly to any of the other sections. Once you have tried adding a hyperlink to a presentation, you'll see how easy (and addictive) it can be.

There are a couple of obvious advantages to using hyperlinks in a computer-driven presentation. One is that it allows you to let the audience set the agenda for your presentation (see the sidebar titled "The Blank Agenda" in Chapter 2). This gives the audience—most often your client—a feeling of empowerment, rather than victimization, during your presentation. The other argument in favor of hyperlinks is that they confer upon you a level of time management that is impossible in a more linear presentation. Few things annoy audiences more than a presenter pounding through slide after slide, saying only, "Well, we don't have time to talk about that, so let's just skip ahead." Adding hyperlinks allows you to skip ahead gracefully and effortlessly, if you need to. You should need to skip ahead only if the level of interaction around an idea is so great that it throws you off your planned schedule—this is a good problem to have.

Know When to Say No

TIP

The most important decision in a computer-driven presentation is to decide whether you need a computer-driven presentation in the first place.

Because of their currency and perceived glamour, computer-driven presentations will continue to be widely used. The important point for a presenter to remember is that the medium should *support* the objective of his or her presentation, not become the objective. So if your objective is to establish rapport, or chemistry, or personal warmth, or to build a relationship, presentation software may be more of a hindrance than a help.

Summing It Up

Presentation software has become an everyday part of the architect's presentation toolkit—so much so that it threatens to displace other tools that may be more appropriate. Using presentation software can add structure and logic to a presentation—an especially helpful advantage if the presenter is somewhat structurally impaired when it comes to presenting ideas in a logical sequence. Some guidelines to keep in mind when using presentation software include:

> ► Use headlines, not sentences, as reminders of what to say.

- Never read bullet points to the audience—this insults their intelligence.
- Opt for a simpler graphic format over more complex and decorative schemes.
- Use subtle transitions, not wild effects, between "slides" and bullet points.
- Never use sound effects, except as a punch line.
- Consider the use of hyperlinks to allow you to move around freely within your presentation.

And after you have followed all the rules for preparing good computer-driven presentations, ask yourself again whether the computer aspect is necessary at all. Remember Marshall McLuhan's dictum that "the medium is the message."

Index

H

Hands, use of, 21
Hostility:
  overcoming irrelevant speeches, 113
  overcoming loaded questions, 115
Hume, David, 35
Humor:
  appropriate, 101–102
  creating, 103
  inappropriate, 100
Humphrey, Muriel, 167

I

Improvisation, 50
Interaction:
  audience, 95
  degree of, 37
  importance of, 38
  interrogation, 97
  maximizing, 39
  overcoming excessive, 119
  team, 96
Inversion Principle, 164

K

Kingwell, Mark, 53

L

Learning objectives, 6
Leave-behinds, 153
Lectern, 23, 24
Light, finding, 69–70

Lighting:
  controlling, 75–78
  worst, where to find, 77
Listening, 145
Location:
  advance viewing, 73
  oversized space, 71
  undersized space, 71
  understanding, 70

M

Manuscript, speaking from, 46
Memorization, 46, 47
Microphones, using, 133–135
Modulation, vocal, 127
Moment, being in the, 145–146, 188
Motivation, 29, 180
Movement:
  orchestrating, 173, 175

N

Notes, use of, 25

O

Objective(s):
  content not in support of, 32
  examples of, 33
  review, 180
  single, 31
Obstacles:
  expectable, 109–111

Presenting:
  Ten Commandments of, 7–9
    success in, 3, 54
  whether to stop, 111–112
Projection:
  audio-visual, 151–152, 200
  vocal, 125–136, 187

R

Reagan, Ronald, 167
Rehearsal:
  helpful, 63–64
  importance of, 59
Research, 55–58
Retrospection, avoiding, 140–142

S

Setting:
  understanding, 69–79, 184
  See also Location
Smalley, Gary, 51
Sound check, 132–133
Speaking opportunities, 60–61
Speech(es):
  methods of, 44–52
  structure of, 64–65
  types of, 30
Stage fright, 117–119
Stage presence, 19
Story line, 34
  elements of, 36

T

Technical problems, overcoming, 117–119
Tension-relaxation exercise, 15
Timing, 168–172, 176
Topic, mastery of, 54
Truman, Harry, 88
Twain, Mark, 57, 172

U

Understudy, need for, 111

V

Visual aids, 149–163
  choosing, 162, 188
  creating, 163
  models, 160
  ownership of, 150
  overheads:
    computer, 157
    traditional, 156
  presentation boards, 155
  relating to, 151
  slides, 158, 189
  video and animation, 160

W

Warming up, 17
Warren, Rick, 38

Z

Ziglar, Zig, 179